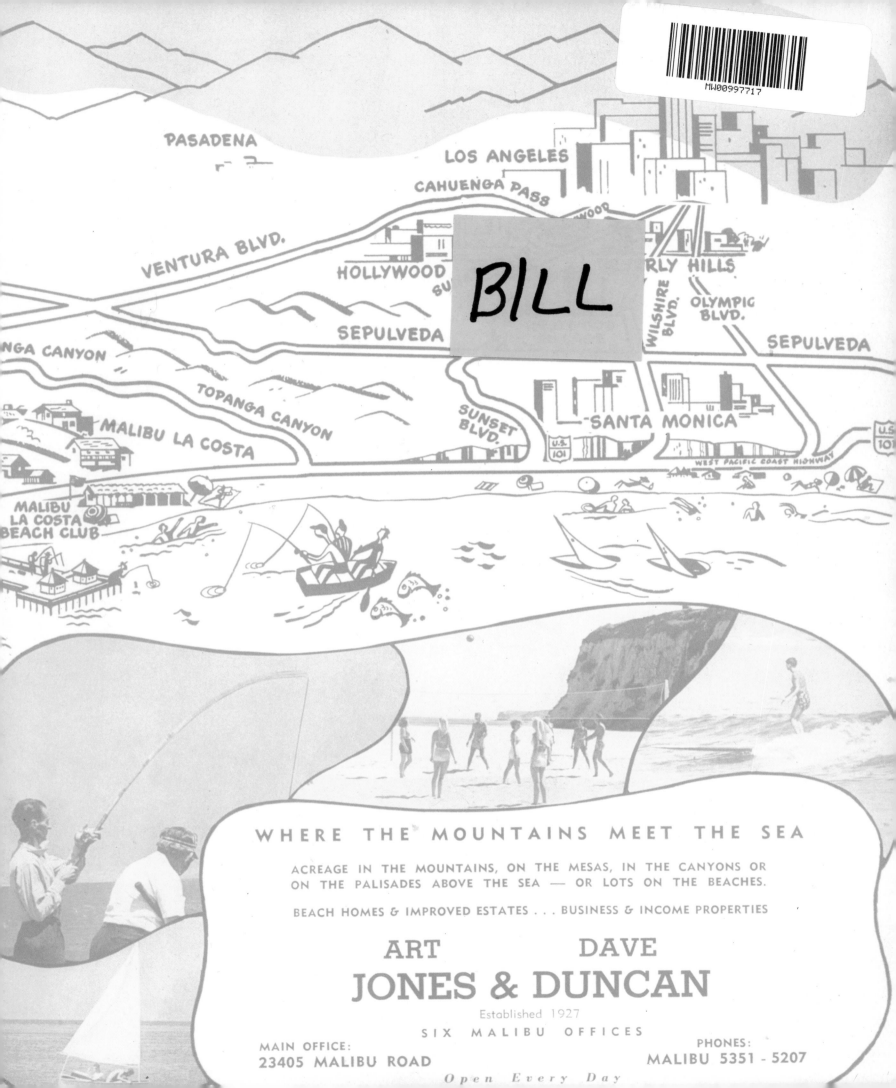

malibu

A Century of Living by the Sea

By Julius Shulman and Juergen Nogai

Introduction by David Wallace

Text by Richard Olsen

HARRY N. ABRAMS, INC., PUBLISHERS

Contents

Acknowledgments Each of the homes featured in this book are lived in by people who have demanding schedules, and each still made time for us to visit them to learn about their unique house and capture it on film for the book. Many friendships were formed along way. Thus, to every one of the homeowners we extend our sincerest thanks and appreciation. ○ Any production such as this that involves a wealth of new photography of private homes cannot be completed without an enormous amount of input from a very patient highly skilled communicator and schedule coordinator. This job was handled with utmost grace by Jeannie Winston Nogai of Santa Monica whose sharpness and easy-going demeanor opened many doors for the book. ○ From start to finish, helping to handle all matter of complicated logistics involved with completing the book was the infallible Judy McKee of Santa Barbara. ○ At Abrams in New York, Sigi Nacson provided copyediting and editorial assistance with her usual steady competence. Graphic designer Brankica Kovrlija sensitively created the beautiful and smart graphic identity of the book. Norman Watkins presided over all printing and production matters with great care and effectiveness. Eric Himmel, publisher, and Harriet Whelchel, managing editor, were a constant source of support and encouragement. ○ Others who contributed in important ways include Malibu musician and designer/builder Randy Nauert, photographer Leroy Grannis, pioneering Malibu surfer, surfboard builder, and architect Matt Kivlin, iconic Malibuite Louis T. Busch, photographer Dan Tompkins, Marc Wannamaker of Bison Archives, Deborah Miller of the Malibu Lagoon Museum, Marsha Feldman of the Santa Monica Mountains Conservancy, and Laura Tate of *The Malibu Times*, who introduced us to the wonderful David Wallace.

—JULIUS SHULMAN, JUERGEN NOGAI, AND RICHARD OLSEN, AUGUST 2004

OPPOSITE, TOP: High tide at Broad Beach, 2004. BOTTOM: Dusk lip dance on a small and atypically private wave at Malibu Point, the spot now called "Surfrider Beach."

Editor's Preface

The idea to make a book that would communicate Malibu's sense of place through a view of its residential-design history occurred to me in 2001, the day I drove out there from Silver Lake to take a quick look at a house near Point Dume by architect Mark Mack. It was a weekday morning, and although traffic wasn't a problem in the direction I was headed, I certainly wasn't alone on the Pacific Coast Highway as I passed through Topanga and into Malibu. However, it did seem that mine was the only vehicle headed in that direction that was not the truck of a contractor. ○ By the time I had progressed another five miles or so, I had counted more than two dozen houses under construction— older homes receiving facelifts along with entirely new ones. Moreover, it had been many years since I was last in Malibu, so even the existing homes were new to me. I started to drive more slowly to get a better look. Some of the houses were disappointing, in many instances caricatures of important historical styles. Others were worse. However, in pointed contrast to these houses was the even greater volume of stunning high-art architecture. ○ The house by Mack was as great as I had been told. Inspired by it and some of the houses I had seen on my way there, I devoted the remaining daylight hours to exploring Malibu more thoroughly.

By sunset, I had covered a lot of ground between the areas of Las Flores and El Matador and along the way had received many stares from homeowners who had caught me admiring their property. In the process of embarrassing myself, however, I had encountered an overwhelming number of great homes created by many of the most established and up-and-coming names in the world of contemporary architecture. In addition to Mark Mack, there was Frank Gehry, Robert A. M. Stern, Richard Meier, Charles Gwathmey, Frank Israel, John Lautner, Jerrold Lomax, Ed Niles, Moore Ruble Yudell, Marmol and Radziner, and Lorcan O'Herlihy. ○ Having seen this magnificent architecture, I had to know more. So I drove straight to Hennessey & Ingalls, the noted architectural bookstore in nearby Santa Monica, to buy a book about Malibu. But I left the store surprised and empty-handed. ○ A year and a half later, I'm back in New York and on the phone with legendary architectural photographer Julius Shulman. Julius, at ninety-two years old, is barely able to hold a conversation with me because his other business lines are constantly ringing and he insists on personally taking every call. Finally, I begin telling him about my concept for the book. I get about two lines into my pitch before Julius completely takes over the conversation,

Malibu's Holiday House Restaurant, 1950, designed by Douglas Honnold. Julius Shulman was hired to photograph it shortly after its completion. In the 1954 edition of *The Malibu*, a handsomely designed and illustrated spiral-bound business guide and directory that was published by Malibuite Lu Mason throughout the 1950s (see p. 8), the Holiday House was one of the featured business entries. "The Holiday House," read the promotional copy, "is internationally known for its excellent cuisine and glamorous atmosphere. The cocktail lounge, with fireplace and piano bar, is a favorite rendezvous for film celebrities."

In 1939, NBC Radio's Arch Oboler of the popular program "Light's Out" commissioned Frank Lloyd Wright to design a series of buildings for a spectacular site high in the Santa Monica Mountains of Malibu. The most substantial of them, a three-level structure with swimming pool that Wright named "Eaglefeather" (1940), was never built. Others were, however, including the Oboler Gatehouse (1940–44), where the Obolers lived for a time, and a cantilevered one-room house called Eleanor's Retreat (1941). As Wright had done only a few years earlier at Taliesin West, the buildings were constructed primarily of local stone and concrete. The Oboler buildings are Wright's only Malibu-based works.

rapidly and lucidly delivering a condensed version of his more than seventy years of memories of this particular place. Soon the project would be up and running, with Julius aggressively leading the way. ○ Julius first started driving out to Malibu from Los Angeles in 1929 when he was a freshman attending the University of California, Los Angeles. As a devoted boy scout of many years, he was at home in the outdoors, and so the pristine natural beauty of early Malibu was a big draw. Often, he would go there alone and explore the landscape and document his findings. As he jokingly described the period, "At that time I was more interested in the birds and bees than the girls." That began to change, however, when he started to receive invitations to Malibu from friends who didn't have cars but did have the girls. Julius would counter such calls with something like, "Well, good, let's go. I'll add those birds to my bird list." ○ Julius was taking pictures then too, using the same Kodak Vest Pocket camera that he used to capture the images of architect Richard Neutra's Kun House that launched his career in 1936. Soon after, he purchased his first Eastman Masterview 4 x 5, which became his primary camera. By 1942, he was in Malibu again, this time as a professional architectural photographer hired to take pic-

tures of an exciting new Modern house for the Clyne family. Those iconic early Shulman pictures of the Clyne House begin on page 66 of the book. ○ Julius has continued to make the journey out to Malibu from his home in Los Angeles, usually with a photographic assistant or an associate, to photograph important new domestic architecture for his clients. Over the course of the past year, working closely with his current associate, veteran photographer Juergen Nogai, Julius photographed more than two dozen houses specially for this book. ○ More than one hundred years of living in Malibu are presented here. The houses are organized by decade, beginning with the first significant domestic-architectural work built in Malibu, the Rindge family's substantial Queen Anne-style home of around 1893. Preceding the tour of homes is David Wallace's look at the history of the place and some of the people who helped shape its identity—a Malibu primer. After this is a photographic tribute to Malibu's golden age of surfing, the 1960s, as captured by Leroy Grannis. Lastly, placed throughout the book are interpretations of the natural side of Malibu, as captured by Julius Shulman and Juergen Nogai. Finally, that book I had hoped to buy is available. — **R. O.**

malibu

Biography of a Challenged Paradise by David Wallace

Malibu, California, is one of the most ballyhooed places in the world, famous from

Arizona to Zanzibar as a fantasyland inhabited by the glamorous, the privileged, and

the lucky. It has been described as: "a state of mind," "a celebrity ghetto," "a way of life,"

and "almost the last ocean frontier." Its name has been used to sell everything from cars

to booze to Barbie dolls. ○ For more than a century, people have been fascinated by the

place. Frederick Hastings Rindge, the man who bought the original Rancho Malibu, which

encompassed much of today's resort community, was among the first to be transfixed.

In 1898 he wrote: "Here in these almost holy hills, in this calm and sweet retreat, protected

from the wearing haste of city life, an ennobling stillness makes the mind ascend to

heaven." For the most part, these descriptions are fairly accurate. The climate is ideal—

generally smog-free and temperate, with an average annual rainfall of fifteen inches.

(Snow is virtually unknown; the last time the beaches were dusted with the white stuff

was in 1989.) Many of Malibu's twenty-seven miles of meandering coastline, sandwiched

between broad beaches fringing the Pacific Ocean and the rugged Santa Monica Moun-

tains, are spectacularly beautiful. Also, Malibu's coast—like that of Santa Barbara's—faces

south, allowing it to be caressed by sunlight from dawn to dusk. And, like the stories say,

on any given day a visitor will probably spot a celebrity going about their business—

shopping, having a hamburger at a popular local restaurant, or visiting their bank.

Another majestic sunset vista from high above (from right to left) Malibu Lagoon, Surfrider Beach, and Malibu Pier, photographed in 2004. The pier, built by the Rindges ca. 1906 to accommodate their personal shipping activity, is one of the defining features of Malibu's built landscape and is set to receive a much-deserved renovation. When the surf is breaking here at Surfrider, traffic in the line up can be as dense and unrelenting as that on the awfully close-by Pacific Coast Highway.

But not all opinions are as gushing. Author Mike Davis, in his book *Ecology of Fear,* dismisses Malibu as the place "where hyperbole meets the surf." Despite his reputation as Southern California's resident critic, he's not altogether inaccurate. Today, despite a modest population of less than thirteen thousand, Malibu is a challenged paradise—a victim of its own popularity. It is a place where weekend traffic often jams the Pacific Coast Highway (PCH), one of the few ways in or out of the community. It is a place where the antiquated septic system adjoining the expensive restaurants and boutiques in the Country Mart shopping center often drains into the high-water table that ebbs and flows with the tide. The result, possibly combined with the discharge from a sewage plant five miles up Malibu Creek, frequently fills the atmosphere with the stench of human waste, and contributes to the occasional pollution of the famous Surfrider Beach and lagoon nearby. "Some days it smells more like Calcutta," says one local.

Malibu's appeal has also had an impact on its once pristine beauty. Paradise Cove was named generations ago because of its crescent-shaped beach of glistening white sand fringed by scrub oak and pine. Today, looking oceanward from the restaurant centered on the cove, the beach still appears pretty heavenly. But look the other way and you will discover a gaudily decked-out (albeit splendidly situated) trailer park. Many of the huge new mansions and condominium developments are also ugly beyond description.

Of course, such problems are encountered by other popular destinations, like Aspen and Santa Fe. But there is another challenge to living in Malibu that can be lethal. Malibu is a battleground for some of nature's most dangerous forces. Parts of the town are damaged—and often destroyed—by flood, landslide, hurricane winds, and Southern California's perennial threat, fire. Sometimes several of these attack at the same time. This potential for disaster is a fact of Malibu life

that motivated Mike Davis to question the sanity of people who choose to live in such a place; he dubbed it "the wildfire capital of North America, and, possibly, the world." Drive just about anywhere and you can find lonely, blackened chimneys—stark, ominous reminders of what will certainly happen again when another conflagration strikes. And, of course, in Southern California, there is the omnipresent threat of a major earthquake.

Nevertheless, the people keep coming. Population pressure continues pushing real estate prices to astronomical levels. (In 2003, a parcel of five forty-foot lots on Carbon Beach sold for sixty-five million dollars; one lot is designated solely for a swimming pool.) Population growth also pushes tempers to incendiary levels. There are the ongoing battles between pro-growth residents and the "keep our town small" people. But, in Malibu, both plans and prejudices are backed with big bucks, and such contests frequently become bitter confrontations. And, just as the potential for natural disasters is a constant physical threat, there is another omnipresent element that affects everyone who owns a home or business here. It's called the California Coastal Commission. Chartered to plan and regulate water and land use in the coastal zone (up to the first mountain-ridge line), the Commission thus controls everything that takes place in Malibu. Put all this together and you have the ingredients for frequent civic chaos. One result: In the entire year of 2003, only a few building permits were issued because of jurisdictional disputes between the state and the community.

Unlike most other popular destinations, because of the high-profile people who live in Malibu, its problems are often played out on a world stage. Consider, for example, if a Roman Catholic resident of, say, Palm Springs, decided that he wanted to follow a pre-Vatican II form of worship, few would care beyond the resort's city limits. But when Mel Gibson, just one of Malibu's many superstar residents, became dismayed over the

TOP: Paradise Cove, ca. 1890; then, truly, an untouched paradise. **BOTTOM:** In June of 1929, a ribbon-cutting celebration marked the opening of the state's Pacific Coast Highway (then called Roosevelt Highway). Passage along the coast from Santa Monica northward to Oxnard was now possible. The floodgates had officially been opened.

changes in the Catholic liturgy, he had the funds to build a church to house his preferred traditional form of worship, and he made news around the world. The same applies to lesser celebrities: In October 2003, when Timothy Treadwell, a Malibu nature photographer and advocate for animal rights, was killed by a grizzly bear on his annual expedition into the Alaskan wilderness, it was carried as a major story everywhere.

Celebrity created today's Malibu, and now Malibu is itself a celebrity.

In *A River Runs Through It*, Robert Redford's 1992 film homage to growing up in Montana in the 1920s, one of the characters exclaims disbelievingly: "I can't picture Ronald Colman riding on a wave!"

She was way out of step with the popular culture of the era.

As a result of Hollywood's domination of the film industry after World War I, by the mid-1920s, moviegoers were fantasizing about American movie stars and their supposedly glamorous lifestyles. Surfing, then a fairly exotic sport that required living in close proximity to warm seas as well as the availability of a lot of free time to spend on a beach, was just the sort of thing fans imagined their idols doing. Along with custom-made cars, luxurious clothes and furs, spectacular homes, and ocean-going yachts, surfing was part of the contemporary daydream fueled by the era's adulatory media. And those daydreams were part of a cultural process that

was for the first time turning stars into "celebrities." Because so many of those early celebrities chose to live (or at least weekend) in Malibu, the place became synonymous with its famous residents.

People who visited Los Angeles in, say, 1930 could see it for themselves. All they had to do was hop in their shiny new Model A and drive a few miles up the Roosevelt Highway (now the PCH) to Malibu. Passing Surfrider Beach, they might have spotted two men in the water, balancing atop huge boards and riding the curls shoreward. Actor Ronald Colman, an early resident of the Malibu Film Colony and a surfing fan, could have been one of them. (Colman's most famous movie was legendary director Frank Capra's 1937 saga *Lost Horizon*; Capra also had a weekend house in the Colony.) The other man could have been the actor's close friend, Duke Kahanamoku, the Hawaiian Olympic-swimming medalist who had earlier introduced Malibuites to the sport. (Kahanamoku also appeared in some thirty films; he costarred with Colman in the 1929 film *The Rescue*.)

Inevitably, celebrity gossip would also fan Malibu's fame. One tale—familiar at the time—also involved Colman. It seems the actor loved to lounge offshore on his yacht, *The Dragoon*. But, as he always worried about missing important telephone calls, he hooked up a light to his telephone that would flash if someone called. (Like today's stars, most of the really important calls were from his agent, proving that there is little

LEFT: A reenactment of Chumash Indians maneuvering one of their finely crafted planked canoes. Like the Indians of other parts of today's United States, the Chumash were eventually driven out by conquerors to make way for "civilized settlement." Fortunately, in today's Malibu—amid all the commerce—the rich culture of the Chumash is a celebrated part of the popular version of Malibu's story. Each year an outdoor festival is held to pay tribute to the Chumash's one-time occupancy of the area. RIGHT: Frederick Rindge's ranchers herding cattle at Ramirez Canyon in 1897.

new under the Malibu sun.) Then he'd jump off the boat, swim ashore, and answer the phone. (In 1940, the year after Vivian Leigh captivated the world as Scarlett O'Hara in *Gone With the Wind*, Colman lent his yacht to her and Laurence Olivier for their honeymoon.)

So why did many celebrities choose to live in Malibu? The answer was location, location, location. Malibu has always been relatively remote from the rest of Los Angeles, ensuring a degree of privacy from adoring fans. Yet it was close enough that one could go back and forth to the studio or the nearby Paramount and Century ranches where hundreds of films were (and still are) made. And if you had a headache, Sunset Boulevard's famous Schwab's Drugstore would even deliver your aspirin to the Colony. Today, although buying toothpaste may be easier, Malibu can still seem pretty isolated, especially during rush hour. But location is still the main reason that dozens of superstars—including Pierce Brosnan, Martin Sheen, Johnny Carson, and Barbra Streisand—continue to live there, maintaining Malibu's indelible association with the mythology of celebrity eighty years after it all began.

Of course, Malibu existed before the celebrities arrived. Although recent research has established that the area was inhabited 4,000 years ago, written history goes back only 462 years when, in 1542, the Spanish explorer Juan Cabrillo anchored at the mouth of Malibu Creek to fill his water casks. There he found a

village called *Humaliwo* by the Chumash Indian inhabitants who fished the local waters in planked canoes. *Humaliwo*, which means something like "where the surf sounds loudly," was soon Hispanicized to *Malibu*.

Another 234 years later the explorer Juan de Anza stopped by and noted little more than that the locals wandered around naked. In 1802 Jose Bartoleme Tapia obtained a concession for farming and cattle grazing on what would be known as the Rancho Topanga Malibu Sequit (such concessions were converted to land-grant ownership only after Mexico, which included California, became independent from Spain in 1822). Three other people owned the property over the next seventy years; the last one, Matthew Keller, bought it in 1857 for fourteen hundred dollars, at a little more than ten cents an acre for the spread. In 1892, his son sold the Rancho for ten dollars an acre to a Massachusetts millionaire (and prohibitionist), Frederick Hastings Rindge, and his wife, May. (Prophetically, the one hundred-fold appreciation in land values over those thirty-five years a century and a half ago is similar to the appreciation of Malibu property during the past three decades.)

With the purchase, Rindge, whose main residence (like most local millionaires of the era) was near downtown Los Angeles, realized his dream to own: "A farm near the ocean, under the lee of the mountains, with a trout brook, wild trees, a lake, good soil, one not too

Rhoda Agatha Rindge and
her father, Frederick,
riding with sheep in Malibu
in the early 1900s.

hot in summer." He built a huge, three-story house as headquarters for his working cattle and grain-raising operation up Malibu Creek and added another thirty-five hundred acres to the property. Six years later, Rindge wrote *Happy Days in Southern California,* in which he recounted the joy of living in a place where the "almost holy hills" edging the Pacific Ocean reminded him of the European Riviera. He was also determined to protect Malibu's natural beauty.

In 1904, the Southern Pacific Railroad decided to link its Santa Monica terminal with its tracks in Santa Barbara, and started proceedings to do so the shortest way possible—directly through Rancho Malibu. Rindge was determined to stop the intrusion and, after discovering a little-known statute prohibiting duplication of existing tracks, confounded the railroad's plan by

starting his own rail line along the coast. The next year he died, reportedly cautioning his widow on his deathbed to protect the unspoiled splendor of their property. For the next two decades May Rindge did so with arrogant determination, building fifteen miles of standard-gauge railroad and fighting off encroachment—especially from the state, which wanted to build a road along the coast—with a battery of lawyers, high fences, and armed riders. Her railroad, grandly dubbed the "Hueneme, Malibu and Port Los Angeles Railroad," was used primarily to transport hides and grain to their private wharf, which survives, in expanded form, as the Malibu Pier. "Hueneme" is the name of a promontory and town that is halfway between Los Angeles and Santa Barbara; the name means "resting place" in Chumash. "Port Los Angeles" was then the name for the

Pacific Electric railroad wharf in Santa Monica. The Rindge's railroad never reached either terminus.

Finally, in 1925, after four state court rulings and two trips to the U.S. Supreme Court, May Rindge was forced to give in. Three years later, the Roosevelt Highway opened to the public. There is an irony in all this. By fighting so determinedly to keep the railroad (and, of course, the public) out of the Rancho and forcing the Southern Pacific to reroute their line around her property, May Rindge effectively preserved the relative wildness of Malibu's charm for future generations of tourists. Her actions also guaranteed that, after the rails for her railroad were removed in the late 1920s, local beach access would remain unspoiled by the railroad tracks that deface the coastline in many Southern California beach communities. (Many rails were subsequently reused as reinforcement in the one-hundred-foot-high dam the Rindges built on Malibu Creek in 1926. Built with no provision for fish passage, the dam

plus downstream pollution have, essentially, rendered extinct the steelhead trout population that once filled Malibu Creek.)

As stubborn as she was, May was smart enough to capitalize on the forced opening of her Rancho. In 1926, she established the Malibu Potteries not far from the pier. For six years—until the Depression—the company turned out brightly colored tiles, thousands of which were used to decorate the Spanish Colonial Revival- and Mediterranean Revival-style houses and public buildings erected all over Los Angeles. The tiles were also used for a pair of murals picturing William Henry Dana's ship, *The Pilgrim*, at San Pedro's Dana Junior High School, and they adorn twenty-three panels in the Los Angeles City Hall.

May Rindge gave her daughter and son-in-law, Rhoda and Merritt Adamson, a thirteen-acre spit of land next to Surfrider's Beach known as Vaquero (Cowboy) Hill. In 1929, on the exact site of the original

The Rindge family in 1900.

Chumash village, the couple built a spectacular home on what was already being ranked among the most valuable pieces of land in the world. Today, run by the state of California as the Malibu Lagoon Museum, the Adamson House remains a well-preserved relic of a vanished way of life. For many years, another reminder of that lifestyle was the presence of the Rindge and Adamson's one-hundred-foot yacht, *The Malibu*, tied up to the Malibu Pier. Built in 1925 of cedar and teak and powered by twin diesels, the yacht was the last word in luxury, boasting three bathrooms, a piano, six staterooms, and a crew of seventeen. Before it was commandeered by the Navy in 1944, the family used it to cruise to Mexico, Canada, and the Caribbean. After the war, it served several decades as a charter boat, and was recently completely restored by its present owners, a Seattle charter service.

In 1924, May Rindge started a private development now known as the Malibu Film Colony, initially renting thirty-foot-wide lots at one dollar per ocean-front foot per month (but tenants had to agree to consume no liquor in their homes). The first person to sign up and build a bungalow (the cost would average twenty-six hundred dollars) was actress Anna Q. Nilsson; Bing Crosby later bought her bungalow. She was soon joined by a "Who's Who" of Hollywood, including the "It girl" Clara Bow, Jack Warner, Harold Lloyd, John Gilbert, and Ronald Colman. Three years earlier, local newspapers had trumpeted the discovery of gold up Trancas Canyon. Nothing much came of it, but it didn't matter. Malibu's gold would be its celebrity residents. "Our family was one of the first to live on Broad Beach," recalls playwright Sandra Heyward, one of Malibu's rare resident natives, and the daughter of Philip Klein, who wrote and produced many of the Shirley Temple and Charlie Chan movies. "My father signed a ninety-nine-year lease with Marblehead Land (the Rindge's real estate company), and built our old-fashioned, brown-

LEFT: Branding cattle at Ramirez Canyon, 1897.
RIGHT: Rindge's ranch hands enjoying a break outside a barn at Malibu Canyon Ranch.

shingle beach house in 1929." According to her father, the Rindges were still running cattle at the time and Bill Steed, the last Rindge foreman, carried a rifle, like May Rindge's armed guards who kept the public out of Rancho Malibu. "No one was allowed to go on the land without permission," Heyward adds.

It wasn't hard for Malibuites to find a drink at the time, despite Prohibition and the Rindge ban on alcohol on their property. All one had to do was hook up with a "rum-runner," many of whom landed booze meant for thirsty Los Angeles in Malibu's Ramirez Canyon, then called "Whiskey Gulch." And, like Prohibition, time would also run out on the Rindge's domination of the community. In December 1940, two months before her death, an impecunious May Rindge was forced to place the Rancho on the auction block. Within six years, 80 percent of the property had been sold.

Although the Great Depression had relatively little impact on Los Angeles (movies provided an escape from economic worries), Malibu remained a rural backwater until after World War II. There was a sheriff's station, and the Malibu Inn, which served as a combination general store, a Greyhound bus stop, and a café. Nevertheless, residents were thinking big. In 1946, before Malibu got local bus service, a post office, or a real school (Webster Elementary replaced the one-room Decker School in 1948), local boosters proposed building a two-million dollar, eleven-acre "yacht harbor"

just west of the lagoon. The plan gathered steam before a group of early environmentalists and the Adamsons, the marina's unwilling neighbors, put a stop to it. (In the 1960s, local environmentalists would also succeed in stopping a freeway, and what was planned to be the largest nuclear power complex in the world. The latter was to include ten nuclear plants to be owned by the Los Angeles Department of Water and Power, the state of California, and Southern California Edison, and was to be built, as discovered after eight years of contentious protest, directly atop an earthquake fault.)

The real event of those years was the war. "Everyone was scared silly by constant rumors of a Japanese invasion," says Heyward. "It was very much like Stephen Spielberg's movie *1941*." "This isn't the state of California," says Robert Stack in the cult film that takes a comic look at the panic that gripped Los Angeles after Pearl Harbor. "This is the state of insanity." People were certain they saw submarines lurking off the coast (apparently only one real one was ever spotted—off Santa Barbara in 1942). "We had an Issei [Japanese-born American immigrant] maid," Heyward recalls, "and whenever she thought she saw submarines in the ocean—which was all the time—she would grab my painting set and write 'I am Issei' in Japanese on Kleenex and wave them in the air."

On Wednesday, February 25, 1942, it seemed that everyone's fears had been realized. At 2:25 A.M. that

TOP: Photographed in 1935, three years before this land became available for purchase, the beach cottage architecture of the Malibu Colony was characterized by its simplicity of form. The average cost of one of these homes was about $2,600. BOTTOM: Like today, the aim of those who retreated to homes in the Malibu Colony in 1939 was largely to gain privacy. Then, there existed in the area little more than a filling station, a market, and only the occasional vehicle passing by on the PCH.

In 1934, the Colony's entrance was as ramshackle as many of its houses.

morning, more than a million Angelenos were wakened by screaming air-raid sirens as radios went silent and the city was blacked out (except for a huge, brilliantly lit sign at the city's port in San Pedro proclaiming "Welcome to Los Angeles" that someone had forgotten to turn off). Twelve thousand air-raid wardens (including Heyward's mother) reported to their posts, and antiaircraft batteries began firing at what appeared to be a large object moving serenely through the beams of searchlights along the coast. The barrage continued for forty-five minutes, raining unexploded shells on roads, houses, and public buildings. "There was an army camp on the cliff right before you turn off to the Bel Air Bay Club in Malibu," Heyward recalls. "They had a World War I cannon, which they fired off during the scare, and the whole cliff fell down, leaving the clearing where a trailer park is today." By dawn the so-called Battle of Los Angeles was over, leaving three people dead of heart attacks and a dairy herd near Malibu wiped out by a wayward shell. No one ever found

out what the mysterious floating object was, although some U.F.O. advocates claim it was a visiting alien spaceship (well, it *is* Los Angeles).

For millennia, far more dangerous to Malibu than any war threats have been the twin plagues of flood and fire. In 1903, sixty-seven years before the famous fifty-room, Mediterranean Revival-style Rindge "Castle" was lost to a later fire, the Rindges were burned out of their first home. In October 1929, a fire destroyed thirteen homes in the Colony. The Decker Canyon fire came exactly a year later, so ferocious that the force of eleven hundred firefighters could only flee for their lives (the conflagration provided the inspiration for the fire that destroys Los Angeles in Nathanael West's *Day of the Locust*). In March 1938, a gigantic storm hit, washing several homes into a raging sea. Local residents, without food, water, or heat, huddled in the courthouse, the Las Flores Inn (now Duke's Restaurant), and director Frank Capra and actress Madeline Carroll were marooned in the Colony for several days. Then, on Christmas Day, 1956, a careless motorist tossed a lit cigarette out of a car into a sixty-mile-an-hour gale. The highly flammable chaparral exploded into a raging inferno, reaching the ocean in many places and creating a holocaust at Broad Beach before firefighters could mobilize. U.C.L.A. librarian Lawrence Powell wrote of the blaze: "God, the whole face of the mountain was burning . . . and moving toward us. Fear dried my mouth. I knew doom when I saw it." Later estimates pegged the wildfire's ferocity as the equivalent of three million barrels of oil burning at two thousand degrees.

By the 1960s, politicians were joining the stars in Malibu. In May 1968, producer John Frankenheimer hosted a beach party for Senator Robert Kennedy, then running for president in the California primary. *Time* magazine reported that, during the party, novelist Romain Gary warned the brother of President John

TOP, LEFT: Charlie Farrell with friends. One of the best-loved actors of the 1930s and a Colony resident, Farrell ended his days in Palm Springs. **RIGHT:** Actress Claire Trevor (right) with friend Olga Melchione on Colony Beach ca. 1934. **BOTTOM, RIGHT:** Circa 1937, starlets Estelle Taylor (left) and Carmen Pantages walked the beach of the Colony. **LEFT:** Just another day at the beach for actress Claire Trevor, who was photographed ca. 1934 while lounging stylishly in the picket-fenced yard of her Colony retreat.

LEFT: Glamour is what brought people to Malibu early on and it still does. In the late 1920s, actress Joan Crawford and Douglas Fairbanks, Jr. (son of the king and queen of Hollywood's golden age the great silent film swashbuckler Douglas Fairbanks and the actress Mary Pickford) were photographed on the Colony beach in their swimsuits. **RIGHT:** Mr. and Mrs. Jascha Heifetz, ca. 1960, preparing to ride the surf. The world's most famous violinist for more than a generation, Heifetz also found the Colony to his liking.

Kennedy, assassinated five years before: "You know, don't you, that someone is going to kill you?" A few days later, during a party at the Ambassador Hotel celebrating Kennedy's primary victory (making him a shoo-in for the Democratic presidential nomination), someone, of course, did.

In the 1960s, like many of the celebrities who lived there, Malibu was becoming the subject of media attacks. Although the community has never had a significant gay population, a 1962 story in *Men in Conflict* by Alexander Rodman asserted: "There is more vice in Malibu than in the rest of America . . . a wide-open sin town [with] a continuous gay parade that simpers . . . across the beaches." Previously, he had attacked Malibu in *Real Men* as, "one of the most degenerate communities in the entire U.S." with "party girls [wearing] nothing at all." The stories prompted a series of vice-squad investigations that concluded that the charges were unfounded and that Malibu was "exceptionally clean." This is not to say that Malibuites were sinless, but in these instances, they were more sinned against than sinning.

Holiday magazine made a more serious attack in May 1969 with their publication of "Welcome to Malibu," a hatchet job written by the bad boy of entertainment journalism, Rex Reed. Reed claimed that "a cesspool of culture empties somewhere in the vicinity of Malibu" and charged that local police "turned on" with hippies

under the pier. But the world didn't care. A place where Rudolf Nureyev taught Barbra Streisand how to dance on the beach on Christmas Day, 1968, was just too glamorous for words.

By 1970, Malibu had changed from the idyllic days of earlier decades. That year, Pepperdine University was dedicated, bringing to the resort not only scholarship but high-profile sports programs, particularly water polo and basketball. Also, the Malibu Civic Center opened, bringing together city and county functions including a court and a branch library in one modernistic, colonnaded complex. And Zuma Beach was "discovered" by Southland surfers, among whom it now enjoys a near-cult status.

Industry, however, arrived a decade earlier in an environmentally friendly way, with the opening of Hughes Research Laboratories' (HRL) first building (the modern building that broods above Malibu atop the ridge line was added in 1989). Now owned jointly by Boeing, Raytheon, and General Motors, HRL is engaged in research related to automotive, space, and defense technology.

As the population grew, homes were built far from the original center of the community near the outlet of Las Flores Canyon. Residents, all within the city limits (the city was incorporated in 1991), could be separated by more than twenty-five miles. The new neighborhoods quickly became identified by their sites:

TOP: The Malibu Inn and, next door, the office of real estate developer Art Jones, photographed in 1944. Jones was the driving force behind the promotion and initial leasing of the lots of the Colony. The landmark Malibu Inn was a center of urban life for a generation of Malibuites and remains among the most popular places in the area.

BOTTOM: Actress Joan Bennett allows a picture of her Colony house living room in 1935. The beach house décor was slightly worn around the edges, but love the stars on the curtains!

Paradise Cove, Trancas (Canyon), and Big Rock. Among them was the promontory named Point Dume, home to such celebrities as Barbra Streisand and Johnny Carson. Pronounced "doom," it was named in 1782 by the English explorer George Vancouver for Father Dumetz, a Franciscan priest he met at the Mission San Buena Ventura.

From the beginning, the population pressure has been on the beachfront property. In 1949, forty-foot-wide lots on Broad Beach, today the residences of such celebrities as Stephen Spielberg and Pierce Brosnan, could be bought for forty-five hundred dollars. Mel Gibson also owns a house on Broad Beach with fireplaces copied from those in the Adamson House. His primary home, however, is in a secluded enclave near the center of town near those of *Titanic* director James Cameron and the late Charles Bronson.

Despite crowning Malibu as "the wildfire capital of North America" Mike Davis intriguingly claims that fire has been at least partly responsible for the astronomical rise in prime Malibu property prices. And it's all the fault of the federal government. "By declaring Malibu a federal disaster area (in the first such ruling by Washington, the Eisenhower administration declared the 1956 Malibu fire a 'national disaster'), and offering blaze victims tax relief as well as preferential low-interest loans," he wrote, "the Eisenhower administration established a precedent . . . [where] each new conflagration would be followed by reconstruction on a larger and even more expensive scale." He concludes: ". . . fire stimulated both development and upward social succession." According to Davis, there's a pot of gold under every burned-out mansion.

But even a cynic would have been challenged by the inferno that started September 25, 1970. Driven by the gale-force Santa Ana winds that bedevil the Los Angeles area every fall, the firestorm roared down Malibu Canyon, past the newly opened Pepperdine

University, taking out the rectory of the adjacent Our Lady of Malibu Catholic Church. After jumping the PCH, it spread both east and west, capriciously destroying over one hundred homes while sparing many neighboring houses. The most celebrated victim of the fire was the Serra Retreat House, originally May Rindge's Mediterranean Revival-style "Castle," sold to the Franciscan order in 1942 for fifty-thousand dollars. Equally devastating was the holocaust's impact on wildlife, especially pets and horses whose numbers had swelled along with Malibu's human population. Three years later another firestorm, less deadly but just as terrifying, swept down Topanga Canyon farther east.

According to some estimates, fires during the last three decades of the twentieth century destroyed more than a thousand homes in Malibu and inflicted more than a billion dollars in damage. The most recent hit Malibu early in November 1993. One resident told the *Los Angeles Times*: "This is hell, dude. I expect to see Satan come out any time now." He and thousands of Malibuites didn't see Satan, but they did see a towering wall of flame roar down Carbon and Las Flores Canyons, where it took out ninety percent of the homes. Jumping the PCH, the conflagration forced the evacuation of many beach houses (a Coast Guard cutter stood offshore ready to evacuate residents). This fire also had its lighter moments: residents fleeing on horseback and roller blades; actors fleeing with Oscars clutched in their arms; a homeowner who leapt into his pool as the fire neared, only to discover a menagerie of local wildlife—raccoons, rats, and a deer—there already. And a pair of women fled out to sea in a kayak with their pets, leaving their maids to fend for themselves. (The homeowners were, appropriately, rescued by hunks from the *Baywatch* TV series; the maids somehow managed to walk out on their own.)

TOP, LEFT: The scene at the Colony following the fire of 1928. **RIGHT:** What burned in the 1928 fire was promptly rebuilt—usually bigger—as Malibuites have done time and time again. When this picture was taken, ca. 1930, the revival styles—Spanish, Anglo-American, English Tudor, and French Manor—were still the most widely accepted images for one's home. Within a decade, however, progressive architecture would find a place here.
BOTTOM, LEFT: Malibu burning. Aerial view of the 1956 fire. Notice the Malibu Pier below the smoke on the left. **RIGHT:** Fire in Latigo Canyon, Christmas, 1956. With Santa Ana winds blowing a raging fire toward you, there is little the fire department can do but tell Malibuites to "Flee!"

With the danger of natural disasters, the crowding, and the pollution of "progress," one might well ask, "why bother with the place?" The best answer is easily discovered. Drive out to Malibu on a fine day—and there are more than three hundred of them annually in Southern California—and take a walk on the beach. If you pick a reasonably remote beach from the two dozen or so within the city limits it may be nearly empty, and the peace and calmness of it all can envelop your spirit like a soft, warm blanket. Frederick Rindge's spiritual stillness still exists. Or follow a road that takes you to the top of one of the local mountains. Then, like the golden eagles that often soar above, look out over Malibu from your lofty perch. The sheer natural beauty of the place will stun you.

"Malibu's biggest challenge is to keep a small town identity against enormous pressures for growth and recreation use which brings in over a million visitors a year," says Arnold York, resident of Malibu since 1976 and publisher of the fifty-eight-year-old *Malibu Times* since 1987 (he also rebuilt his home after losing it in the 1993 fire). "Malibu's remoteness is still the greatest part of its attraction which gives people who choose to live here a feeling of safety as well as—especially for the celebrities among us—privacy. Malibu's beauty is one thing. But there is another important attribute—its people. Rarely have I come across a community with a greater number of talented, creative individuals. And they also possess a unique sophistication; ask any celebrity, and one of the things they like best about Malibu is the habit of leaving celebrities alone which goes all the way back to the early days of the film colony. People, famous or not, don't like to live behind walls all of the time. They like to live like real people. And, in Malibu, for the most part, they still can."

"Malibu, January 1960. From my mountain nook I can see Palos Verdes, Catalina Island, Santa Barbara Island, Ana Capa, and Santa Cruz Islands. It's the best frontier, and they're moving in fast."

—TOM BLAKE, who in 1926 (with Sam Reid paddling out beside him) became the first person ever to surf Malibu, writing to friend and fellow surfer Tom Zahn

ABOVE: Surfrider Beach in the summer of 1962. Following the 1959 release of the film version of *Gidget*, water traffic here would forever be a problem.

OPPOSITE, TOP: During the 1960s, noseriding master Lance Carson (b. 1943) may have slept and collected his mail at his Pacific Palisades address, but the rest of the time he was most likely to be found gliding across the best waves of the day at Surfrider Beach. BOTTOM: Matt Kivlin (b. 1929), Dewey Weber (1938–1993), and most of the other surfers pictured in the book would have to be an integral part of any serious discussion of, or in this case tribute to, Malibu's golden age of surfing. So would Johnny Fain (b. 1943), shown here bottom turning on a mellow day at Malibu. Among the small group of truly dominant Malibu surfers of the 1960s, Fain, whose family was in the movie business, was the only one who lived in the Colony. When Fain was on a wave, people watched, whether for his ability to generate great turning speed, or for pulling moves like the handstand just to keep onlookers stoked. "He was one of my favorite surfers," said legendary surf photographer Leroy Grannis.

Surfrider Beach, August 1963.

Though a resident of San Diego, the highly influential Mike Hynson (b. 1942) made the trek to Malibu often in the early 1960s, both for contests (he placed fourth in the Malibu Invitational of 1963) and for free surfs. Hynson was known as a supreme stylist, and Malibu's point break suited him perfectly. "He was one of the sport's great masters of trim, often letting his board run on a straight, elegant line," wrote surf historian Matt Warshaw in his 2003 book *The Encyclopedia of Surfing*. Hynson doing his thing at Surfrider in August of 1961, a couple of years before beginning an around-the-world journey as part of Bruce Brown's 1966 genre-defining surf film *Endless Summer*.

OPPOSITE: During the 1960s, the wall at Surfrider Beach, shown here in July of '64, often received artfully inscribed declarations from admirers of Miki Dora.

ABOVE: The father of modern surfing, Duke Kahanamoku (1890–1968), standing next to the surfer whose personal style in and out of the water is largely responsible for Malibu's mythical status in the surfing world from the late 1950s onward, Miki Dora (1934–2002). Dora receives a handshake from the Duke after taking his trophy at the International Surfing Hall of Fame induction ceremony of 1966.

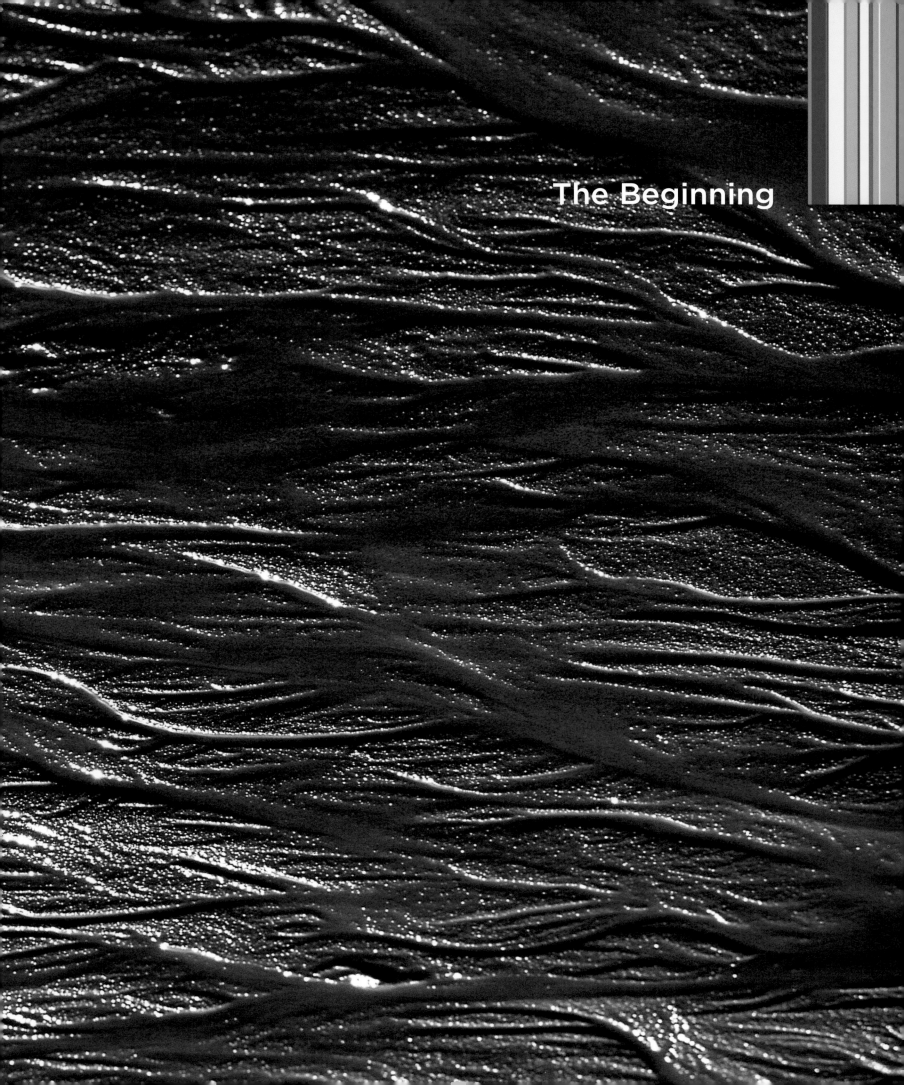

The Beginning

A HOME ON RANCHO MALIBU

Rindge House, ca. 1893

In Malibu, the notion of using high-art architecture to make a public statement about one's achievements or social status is an old tradition. It began with the construction of this home, built around 1893. In 1892, Frederick Hastings Rindge acquired the 13,315-acre Malibu ranch and began planning the house that would grace the property he had fallen in love with. ○ As a native of Cambridge, Massachusets, and a member of a socially elevated family, Rindge was familiar with the fashionable architecture of the day, particularly that of the elite resort destination of Newport, Rhode Island. In fact, it is said that throughout this period Rindge continued to vacation at a retreat in Marblehead, Massachusetts, where he would have been further exposed to the latest East Coast architectural trends. In Newport, architect Henry Hobson Richardson had built the trendsetting William Watts Sherman House (1874–75), regarded by many as the first American example of Queen Anne-style domestic architecture. (English architect Richard Norman Shaw (1831–1912) is the style's actual originator.) As it did for many other wealthy individuals at the time, the Watts Sherman House would have left a lasting impression on Rindge. On the exterior, Richardson sheathed the asymmetrical three-story volume in exposed half-timbers and decorative brick and stucco infill, with additional touches of terra cotta cresting and quarry-faced masonry. The opulent interior, largely the work of artists and designers including Louis Comfort Tiffany, John LaFarge, and Stanford White, featured elaborate carvings, paintings, tilework, and stained glass. The house epitomized the idea of hand-crafted expression. ○ Within a decade of the Watts Sherman House's completion, Queen Anne, whether in its high-art or more modest vernacular incarnations, would become the dominant architectural style for homes across America. Then, the most spectacular example in Los Angeles was the Bradbury House of 1890. Rindge's three-story house in Malibu was built at a time when the Queen Anne's popularity was beginning to wane and the Anglo Colonial Revival style was gaining in favor and bears hallmarks of both styles. Dominant features are the Queen Anne's highly complicated roofline with multiple gables, turret, elaborate wraparound porch with decorative balustrade, decorated cornices and bargeboards, wall surfaces decoratively finished in a variety of materials (including brick and shingle), and tall chimneys ribbed in the Elizabethan tradition. But also present are the elaborate porticos that would later be a defining feature of the Colonial Revival-style house. Like many great Malibu houses that would follow it, however, the spectacular Rindge House was destroyed by fire, taken from the Rindge family in 1903.

1920s

Fazenda House, ca. 1924

It is difficult to give an exact date of construction to the house of actress Louise Fazenda (1895–1962) because records from the period are non-existent. Two notable and verifiable facts are the thirty foot size of Fazenda's lot, and that she was responsible for getting the house designed and built on the site she leased from May Rindge. ○ Given the architectural complexity and refinement of certain houses built for actors like Fazenda during this very same period in Santa Monica, for instance, one can surmise that because of the lease-only arrangement offered by the Rindges, Fazenda deemed it impractical to build anything other than a no-frills beach shack. Thus, Fazenda's Colony house, raised about a foot off the sand on blocks, was given a simple hip-and-valley roof, board-and-batten sheathing (like the modest working buildings on the nearby Rindge ranch), fireplace, small porch, and windows running the perimeter of the house to take in the then unobstructed views. An outbuilding appears in the background. However modest, the house would have made a great quick getaway for a busy actress like Fazenda, who in 1924 appeared in seven pictures, including *The Galloping Fish* and *The Lighthouse by the Sea*.

Colman House, ca. 1926-27

Ronald Colman's first Colony beach house was under construction around the very time that Tom Blake (1902–1994) and Sam Reid (1905–1978) became the first surfers to ride Malibu Point. Colman was also an avid surfer, and as a friend of Duke Kahanamoku (1890–1968), with whom he appeared in a number of films, he would have had received instruction from the best in the world. ○ The house is remarkable perhaps only in its form, which is nearly identical to Louise Fazenda's house. This suggests that it could have been a standard model offered by local builders. In Colman's version, however, redwood shingles replace the board-and-batten finish, the substructure is concealed, the corner porch is partially enclosed and given windows, and a lamp is attached to the gable end. Unlike Fazenda's property, there are other homes at either side of the Colman House, suggesting an age difference between the two houses.

Adamson House, 1929 Stiles O. Clements, Architect

The house that was built on the land between the lagoon and the pier, right at the point next to Surfrider Beach, for Frederick and May Rindge's daughter Rhoda and her husband, Merritt Huntley Adamson, is a fine example of the Spanish Colonial Revival style merged with certain distinguishing characteristics (such as the window shapes) borrowed from Moorish design. With features that include hand-painted murals, lead-framed bottleglass windows, hand-wrought ironwork, and carved teakwood doors, along with the undeniable architectural pedigree of being a Stiles O. Clements design, the Adamson House would have been regarded as a work of importance. Moreover, inside and out, adorning a portion of nearly every surface of the home and its garden structures is brilliant decorative glazed tile made by the Rindge's Malibu Potteries. The house is, in effect, a habitable monument to some of the finest decorative tilework produced in California in the twentieth century. ○ By the time Clements's design began to take its final shape at the drafting board, Malibu Potteries, at one time located only a half-mile east of the pier on Carbon Beach, had established itself as a major designer and producer of decorative ceramic tile of a quality that was unrivaled in the United States at the time. The work of the firm, which remained in operation only from 1926 until 1932, continues to be passionately collected. Today, the Adamson House, filled with many of the family's original furnishings, is carefully preserved as part of the Malibu Lagoon Museum.

1930s

Fazenda House II, ca. 1930

In most European countries, when one builds a house it is meant to sustain a generation or more of use in its original form. This is not so in America, and especially in Malibu. We have a long-standing tradition of creative reinvention, particularly when it comes to our homes. ○ At an undocumented point between 1924 and 1930, actress Louise Fazenda gave her Colony beach house a complete makeover. A careful comparison of the photographs of the two houses reveals that each shares the same structural features and ground-floor massing, among other telling details. In each house, observe the positioning of the chimney and the fenestration on the left side of the house in relation to the positioning of the front left corner and back end. The first-floor window at the right side of each house is also in the same position in relation to the entryway. Also consider the positioning of the skyline of the mountain range behind both houses. ○ After several years there, Fazenda could have out-grown the rusticity of the original house and decided to reinvent it as a Tudor Revival, complete with the characteristic decorative half-timbering with white stucco infill and a roof finished with hexagon-shaped composition shingles. The rest of the stylistic signs of the Tudor image were omitted, though it probably didn't matter to Fazenda or her house guests.

Bow/Bell House, 1933

The house of Brooklyn-born actress Clara Bow (1905–1965), early Hollywood's "It" girl, and Rex Bell (1903–1962), one of the most famous early movie cowboys and later the Lieutenant Governor of Nevada, is another example of Hollywood's willingness to live without architectural distinction in order to be part of the fashionable Colony set on the beach at Malibu. While drab and undistinguished, the house symbolizes an important chapter in the evolution of the Colony's architecture. At this time, its lots and the houses on them were still only for lease. Soon, however, houses like this would receive the full brunt of Hollywood's aesthetic scorn, the momentum of which had been accruing throughout the lease-only period. A race to remove such eyesores to make way for luxurious "personal statement" homes was not far off.

Baxter House, ca. 1934

Warner Baxter (1889–1951), an Oscar winner for his performance as the Cisco Kid in 1929's *In Old Arizona* and one of the highest paid actors of his time, surely was accustomed to grander accommodations than this feeble attempt at a Monterey Revival-style house at the Colony. In 1934, when this photograph was taken of Baxter nattily attired in his bathing suit, the Malibu beach house was the embodiment of architectural modesty. Actors like Baxter roughed it when they were at their beach houses in Malibu. It was necessary if they were to be part of the happening scene of the Colony, and Baxter was known to be a Malibu fixture.

Even in the early 1930s, with the Great Depression requiring frugality for many, some Malibuites would not settle for a single-lot property. Less was never more here. Sylvia Sidney (1910–1999) came to Hollywood via her native Bronx, New York, and within a few years became a sensation for her work in the Paramount film *City Streets* (1931). As film historian and critic Leonard Maltin has pointed out, in terms of her stature in the business Sidney replaced the great Clara Bow. ○ Evidently, the star of *Ladies of the Big House* (1931) needed more space for her Colony home than the standard thirty-foot lot. As a major Hollywood player and the lover of Paramount executive B. P. Schulberg, she had no trouble getting it. ○ The relatively handsome two-story Colonial Revival-style house,

which boasted a courtyard with gardens and potted shrubs and trees below its wraparound balcony, was finished on the exterior in white clapboard with fixed shutters for decorative effect. Adding to its attractiveness, planters were attached to the ground-floor window aprons of the beachfront elevation. The generous porch space, nearly the width of Clara Bow's entire house, was finished with picture windows and a glass-paneled door. Above was a similarly proportioned open deck space. Also noteworthy is the manner in which the property met the beachfront. In place of the typical picket fence, common in so many other Colony homes of the period, Sidney's house was separated from the sand and surf by a solid three foot wall, giving the property a more finished look and

pronounced sense of security. ○ Inside the home, Colonial Revival-style furnishings dominated the living space. The bead-jointed plank walls were painted bright white, as were the exposed ceiling beams. In the hearth area, considered the heart of any proper Colonial Revival-style house, sat a spinning wheel—perhaps an antique. Directly above, an exaggerated scroll-sawn fireplace surround supported a small cuckoo clock, another common Colonial Revival decorative object. In the corner of the living room, next to the built-in window seat, was Sidney's desk and Windsor chair. On the floor, Sidney had a braided rug—the Colonial Revival-style finishing touch that had been made essential a decade earlier by Early America promoter Wallace Nutting.

1940s

Clyne House, 1942

The spectacularly sited Clyne House, an example of the kind of "moderate Modernism" that was finding acceptance with a small portion of the home-buying public in the early 1940s, represents a great leap forward in terms of Malibu beach house architecture. To build such a house at this time, the Clynes had to be progressive thinkers. As the late architectural historian Esther McCoy wrote of these years, "The clients of modern houses were often professional people with moderate incomes—progressives, they were called. Perhaps because they saw the need for change in their own fields—education, law, medicine, politics, the arts—they were receptive to change in architecture." ○ By 1938, the lease-only terms of the Colony were no longer in effect. Land could now be purchased through Rindge's Marblehead Land Company. Homes no longer had to be sited directly on the beach in the Colony's small lots, which of course completely altered the dynamic of the Malibu lifestyle. By 1942, Malibu was slowly becoming a getaway destination for families like the Clynes. ○ While generally Modern in form, the Clyne House's detailing is quite rustic. Like the many Ranch House-style homes that would soon be built in Malibu by designer Cliff May and others, board-and-batten sheathing was used, and traditional bay windows were incorporated into the design instead of floor-to-ceiling glass walls or sliding doors. The carriage porch is perhaps the most unusual element of the design, lending a sense of formality to what is otherwise an informal vacation home for a small family.

Murphy House, 1946 Griswold Raetze, Architect

Five years before the completion of this house, its designer, Griswold Raetze (1910–unknown), was earning a living not as an architect, but as a set designer in the art department of Metro-Goldwyn-Mayer Studios in Culver City. Raetze's career took a turn when in the fall of 1941 his boss, Cedric Gibbons, hired a young Midwesterner to the position of staff architect. His name was Charles Eames. Raetze would soon learn that Eames and his wife, Ray, had been working intensely on a concept for molded-plywood chair seats and had presented a molded-plywood leg splint to the U. S. Navy for possible use. When the Navy finally accepted the Eames's prototype in the summer of 1942, Charles left the job at MGM Studios in order to devote all of his time to the molded-plywood work, taking two of his MGM design colleagues with him, one of whom was Raetze. Together, they formed the Plyformed Wood Company (later called Evans Products), located initially on Santa Monica Boulevard. Raetze continued to work for Eames as the company evolved. He left at the end of 1946, the year the Murphy House in Malibu was finished. o The Murphy House is significant as an early example of high-art Modern architecture in Malibu. As Julius Shulman recalls of his first visit to the home, "Raetze designed the house for a motion-picture director. It was evident on viewing the house that Murphy's level of taste exceeded that of the majority whose Malibu homes were more akin to 'play houses' than serious architecture. The house was removed from the oceanfront, affording more open vistas of the coastline and greater privacy. The trelliswork on the overhangs was inspired by some of Richard Neutra's early designs." o Raetze gave the house a gently pitched flat roof and floor-to-ceiling glass walls that wrapped around the corners of the beachfront elevation. Between the two wings that reach toward the ocean (living room at right, bedroom at left) was the kitchen and, adjacent to it, a stone-paved patio space. Direct access to the patio from the kitchen and living room was made via Dutch doors, and an outdoor barbeque compartment was part of Raetze's design for the broad chimney. o Inside the house, the living room featured abundant built-in shelving along the wall opposite the attractive fireplace. As was customary at the time for a modern house, the built-in unit was constructed of plywood, without any decorative flourishes. The paneled walls, like the ceiling beams, were given a natural finish.

Becket Beach House, 1948 Welton Becket, Architect

With the completion of architect Welton Becket's (1902–1969) Malibu beach house in 1948, word had spread that Malibu was becoming a place for serious architecture. That same year, the highly influential Modernist Richard Neutra (1892–1970) had completed a house in nearby Pacific Palisades for *Arts & Architecture* magazine's Case Study program as well as a major portion of his contribution to Malibu's Holiday House Restaurant and Hotel complex—a series of sleek balconied apartments that had been placed dramatically at the edge of a cliff overlooking the Pacific. Like Neutra, Becket was known for modern work of an exceptionally high level of refinement. His firm, Wurdeman and Becket, had designed some of the Los Angeles area's most

iconic buildings to date, including the Streamline Moderne-style Pan-Pacific Auditorium in Hollywood (1935), the hugely promoted prototype Modernist home called The Postwar House in Beverly Hills (1946), and the International Style Bullock's in Pasadena (1947). At the time of his death, Becket's office was the largest architectural practice in the world. ○ For his family's beach house, Becket concentrated on vistas, giving the beachfront elevation a wall of fixed glass that spanned the full width of the house. Glass doors connected the flowing straight-line open plan of the two-bedroom interior living space with a concrete patio area that extended toward the beach in accord with the roof overhang, lending at least partial shade to the southern exposure. Ribbon

windows were used along the street elevation, lighting the kitchen and allowing views of the mountains to the north. Where glass wasn't used, walls were finished in sand-colored brick that gave the house privacy while at the same time uniting it with its site. Becket also designed a glass windshield that reached out from the western-most corner of the beachfront elevation onto the sand, shielding a narrow pathway that connected the house to a separate glass-enclosed patio room for entertaining on the beach. ○ On the day that photographer Julius Shulman visited the house, Becket had family and friends there. In the photograph taken from the patio room, Becket is seated at right. The children in the photographs are the Becket children.

Medford House, 1954 Kenneth Lind, Architect

The two-story Medford House is another example of the regionalist-Modern wood post-and-beam construction that would be popular in Malibu throughout the 1950s. The Medfords had purchased a small lot but required a large house— ample enough to accommodate various entertainment functions and the demands of an active family. They also wanted the home to have a swimming pool. Architect Kenneth Lind (1909–1975), who had received a national design award from *Progressive Architecture* magazine in 1948, responded with a highly effective plan that focused on free-flowing space and bringing the outdoors in. ○ Lind gave the house a dramatic point of entry via a double-height foyer, partially walled in glass. Just beyond the glass was a

patio and swimming pool that began outside uncovered before gracefully meandering into the house to connect with an atrium, where a small garden was kept. Sunlight would reflect off the pool and dramatically fill the foyer. He then took the concept of the typical open plan and pushed it a little further, containing the home's living room, dining room, and kitchen in a single open space without any screens or dividers. Cork tiling was used on the floors throughout, which was effective at absorbing noise from the surf, and the living room featured tongue-and-groove cladding and sliding glass doors that connected it to the broad cantilevered deck off the back of the house. Besides unobstructed views of the ocean, the focal point of the living

room was the "feature fireplace" done in the shape of an upside-down cone. By the early 1950s, the freestanding fireplace had become a major selling point of the Modern home. It would remain popular for the next decade. In her 1994 book, *Contemporary: Architecture and Interiors of the 1950s*, architectural historian Lesley Jackson described the typical treatment of this unique feature: "Often free-standing in the manner of a stove, the fireplace was treated as an independent art object, on a par with a piece of modern furniture or sculpture, rather than as part of the physical structure of the building." The bedrooms were placed on the second floor, with the master having sliding glass doors that led to the room's own spacious sun deck.

Wing House, 1957 Carl Maston, Architect

In mid-1950s Los Angeles, if one were seeking an architect to create a house that would epitomize the most current notion of high-art architecture, or more specifically, the International Style, one could not find a more capable designer than Carl Maston (1921–1992). By the time he was approached by the Wings, Maston had completed two important residential works, his own house in West Hollywood (1948) and the Herman House in Brentwood (1948). His Dunham House in Pasadena (completed in 1956) was in progress. Each of these homes received substantial press coverage as well as various citations for design excellence. O For his first commission in Malibu, Maston designed a home with a deceptively simple street-facing facade. It consisted of two seemingly independent flat-roofed wings that intersected at the point of entry to form the shape of an L. The projecting wing contained the garage and, behind it, service areas, bath, and fitted kitchen. The receded second wing, which was lower in height in order to accommodate light-giving clerestories at its juncture with the other wing, reached horizontally across the back end of the house's expansive entry court and contained the living and dining room, bedrooms, and an additional bath. O In striking contrast to the front elevation, the back of the house, which looked out to a ravine leading to the ocean, was given a monumental central pavilion supported by white-enameled structural steel, which likely would have been inspired by Mies van der Rohe's 1951 Farnsworth House in Plano, Illinois. Deeply receded beneath the pavilion were floor-to-ceiling fixed and sliding glass panels that brought abundant breezes, sunlight, and dramatic vistas to the large living and dining space.

1960s

Copeland–Waycott House, 1963 Cliff May, Designer

As the 1960s took hold in Malibu, the most popular image of home, other than Modern, was the Ranch House that drew inspiration from notions of the Old West. One designer in particular was largely responsible for its proliferation. Working mostly with architect Chris Choate, Cliff May (1908–1989) had achieved enormous success designing homes in the Ranch mode across the country. As opposed to the relatively simple Ranch House type that was fast becoming the dominant offering in tract developments across the United States, May's Ranch houses were stylized, done mostly in the Spanish hacienda tradition. However, as architectural historian Alan Hess highlighted in his 2004 book *The Ranch House*, the general plan utilized by May was not new to Southern California: "The hacienda plan—with outdoor and indoor spaces overlapping—showed up in the Greene's 1903 Bandini House, Henry Greene's 1913 Crowe House, Schindler's 1921 Kings Road House, Roland Coate's 1925 James K. Tweedy House in Downey, California, in the car court of William Wurster's 1927

Gregory Farmhouse, as well as May's first speculative houses in 1932." May added his own spin, the specifics of which he outlined in two books, *Sunset Western Ranch Houses* (1946) and *Western Ranch Houses by Cliff May* (1958), both published by the San Francisco-based *Sunset* magazine. ○ In the first book, May laid out a set of selling points for the Ranch House, one of which stated that there should not be a "front" or "back" to the house. This particular concept is one of the most noticeable characteristics of the stucco and board-and-batten sheathed U-shape house he designed for this hilltop site in Malibu. Entry to the house is made through one of its multiple sets of substantial handcarved mahogany doors that original owner Copeland had acquired from a craftsman in Mexico. They lead to a spacious central courtyard, the perimeter of which is covered by another typical May design feature, a corridor, or as he enticingly described it, an "open-air hallway and sheltered lounging area." From the courtyard, formal entry to the interior spaces

is made through another set of carved mahogany doors that open to the living room. Here, one can see many of May's signature touches at work including plank ceilings with a metal skylight extending the full length of its ridge, exposed board-and-batten walls (the bats are rough hewn), multiple sliding glass doors giving easy and wide access to the courtyard, and a massive brick fireplace, a feature that originally would have included a pot hook and barbeque. Next to the fireplace, May placed an additional set of sliding glass doors that lead to a large patio and rose-filled garden space and permit views of the adjacent corral and, beyond it, the Pacific Ocean. ○ Today, the house retains most of its original May-designed features. When they purchased the home, the present owners were appreciative of May's work, and thus the updates that were made to the house, including modernizing the kitchen and changing the cedar shakes to fire-resistant composite shingles, were done sensitively.

LeBrun House, 1966 Thornton Abell, Architect

Santa Monica architect Thornton Abell (1906–1984) was one of eight architects chosen in 1945 to participate in *Arts & Architecture* magazine's Case Study House program (1945–1967). In 1948, Abell produced Case Study House #7 in San Gabriel, a design that received considerable critical acclaim. By the year that he began working on the Malibu home for the LeBrun family, he had completed several highly regarded works, among them the Haines House (1951) in Pacific Palisades, the Ullman House (1955) in Santa Monica, and, in Brentwood, the Leslie House (1950) and his own award-winning office building (1954). Throughout his long career Abell remained a staunch Modernist whose designs always embraced the outdoors. The house he finished in 1966 in Malibu is a reflection of that sensibility. ○ The LeBrun House was sited on a large lot close to Zuma Beach, not far from the Pacific Coast Highway. Abell's plan set the house at the back of the property for greater privacy. He gave it a flat roof and poured-in-place concrete walls that had a wood-grain textured surface—a decorative effect—as a result of the builder's use of boarded formwork. (An intentional design strategy that gives the bare concrete surface a three-dimensional, shadow-casting effect, this look had achieved popularity for residential use, at least among Modernist architects like Abell, after leading Modernist architect Le Corbusier appropriated it in several of his works, including the enormously influential Unite d'Habitation apartment complex in Marseilles, France, in the late 1940s.) While aesthetically cold to many observers, concrete walls, besides being strong and resistant to fire, require no paint and virtually no maintenance, even in a coastal climate, which would have helped Abell sell this particularly progressive part of the design to the LeBruns. ○ The LeBruns required a house that would accommodate living and working functions, and Abell responded by giving each its own wing. At the front, where the two wings met, formal entry to the house was made dramatic by requiring passage through a walled and thoroughly planted court with a reflecting pool. Below extended eaves, floor-to-ceiling fixed glass panels on the facade enabled a strong visual connection between the pool and surrounding plantlife and the interior of the living-space wing. There, contained in a single large volume, was the living room with its poured-concrete fireplace, an informal dining area, and the ribbon-windowed kitchen, the latter separated from the other functions only by a counter with a floating cabinet positioned a few feet above it. Sliding glass doors easily opened this part of the house to a generously proportioned outdoor room with trellis, an extension of the primary living space.

Stevens House, 1968 John Lautner, Architect

The highly unconventional Stevens House in the Colony is the first Malibu house of architect John Lautner, one of the twentieth century's most extraordinarily gifted and experimental designers of houses. Lautner (1911–1994) began his architectural experience in 1933 as an apprentice to Frank Lloyd Wright. He had joined Wright's Taliesin Fellowship, a unique live-in educational program for aspiring architects that Wright and his third wife, Olgivanna, had launched from their Spring Green, Wisconsin, home (also called Taliesin) only a year before Lautner's arrival. The young Lautner would spend five years with the Wrights as a member of the Fellowship, living under the influence of the highly creative and strong-willed Mrs. Wright and working directly under the master on some of his major projects of the time including the Roberts House (1937) in Marquette, Michigan, a house commissioned by Lautner's own mother-in-law, the house known as Wingspread (1937) in Wind Point, Wisconsin, and Taliesin West (1937) in Scottsdale, Arizona. ○ In 1938, Lautner left the Fellowship to work on his own in Los Angeles, though he would remain a trusted and respected affiliate of Wright for years to come, working,

mostly in a supervisory role, on Wright's Los Angeles-based projects such as the Sturges House (1939) in Brentwood. In 1940, Lautner finally realized his first independent work, a house built in Silver Lake for himself and his family. ○ Throughout the next quarter century he would even break the mold created by America's most famous architect, routinely stretching the perceived boundaries of his teacher's concept of organic architecture. If at this time one was to hire Lautner, one would get an inventive free-form expression of anything but the commonly held notion of what a house should look like. As Alan Hess wrote in his book *The Architecture of John Lautner* (1999), "Of all the architects who passed through Wright's sphere, only R. M. Schindler, Bruce Goff (who never studied or worked with Wright), and Lautner managed to drive Wright's ideas beyond the master." Most of Lautner's works were located in Southern California. ○ Constructed on one of the Colony's challenging narrow lots (thirty-two feet wide in this case), the Stevens House accommodates a surprisingly large number of functions. Lautner placed a maid's room with its own bathroom, a children's playroom, and a studio

below grade and gave them a separate entrance. The ground-floor level was dedicated to the living room and dining area, the latter closer to the front of the house but raised enough to give it clear views of the ocean beyond the living room. A partially covered lap pool was tucked tightly into a narrow space just between the floor-to-ceiling glass walls of the living room and the roof, which actually touched the sand. Along with the master bedroom, which also had direct views of the pool and the ocean through floor-to-ceiling glass, the children's bedrooms were fitted into the top floor. ○ In his book *John Lautner, Architect* (1994), a project completed just before his death, Lautner wrote, "A lot of this size has always been the same: impossible! My first bout with the site and the requirements made me aware of just how difficult it would be to put all desired rooms and spaces on this property, particularly considering building setbacks and height limits. A prior architect had given up on including a pool. When I was first called in, I asked the owner to avoid telling me what he had heard, but rather to express his needs, whatever they might be. He did so, and I went to work on them."

1960s 107

Brown House, 1969 Buff and Hensman, Architects

Buff and Hensman's award-winning architectural partnership was formed in 1949, a few years before they both were asked to join the staff of their alma mater, the architecture school of the University of Southern California (USC). Conrad Buff III (1926–1988) and Donald Hensman (1924–2002) were Modernists—they had been chosen to design two houses for *Arts & Architecure* magazine's Case Study program—but in the so-called soft Modern sense. (They didn't see the chilly steel-and-glass-box aesthetic of their purist contemporaries as the only answer to an architectural challenge.) Like so many other Modernist architects who began working in Los Angeles in the 1950s, Buff and Hensman had begun to look closely at the Craftsman Style houses of Charles Greene and Henry Greene, including the Greenes' wood masterpiece, the Gamble House (1908) in Pasadena. Soon, wood, often darkened with stain, would be their primary building material, and many of their houses, though still largely in a Modern idiom, would be given Craftsman styling. ○ At the end of the 1960s, attitudes toward the stereotypical Modern box were changing in favor of a more nostalgic architecture. Leading Craftsman historian Robert Winter touched on this subject in his book *Craftsman Style* (2004), noting that, "As criticism of modernist architecture increased in the 1960s, the Craftsman tradition was revived, especially in California and sometimes within the modernist camp

itself." ○ Buff and Hensman's design for the Browns' small Malibu beachfront lot was generally Modern in terms of its spatial arrangement and form, but it had a woodsy appearance that softened its geometry and blended it with nature. The three-bedroom, two-bath, two-story house was raised off the sand on massive stained wood beams connected to concrete-and-steel piles, removed from the threat of high surf. The house was sheathed in cedar shingles that had been left natural to acquire a patina that would contrast with the large tinted glass panels of the facade and the dark stained wood that framed the house. A small fenced-in court paved in quarry tiles made private the glass-walled entry that was receded behind the garage wall, pushed further back from the noise and activity of the street. In order not to obstruct views of the ocean from the double-height foyer, the front-of-the-house access to the second floor was made via a spiral staircase, instead of an enclosed form. The formal entry was further connected to the ocean views at the house's back by running the clay-colored floor tiling of the front court through the foyer and dining area and out to the beach-facing sun deck. Directly above the deck, on the side of the house that contained the shag-carpeted sunken living room, was a partially covered balcony that extended the master bedroom space outside through sliding glass doors, giving it an excellent view of Malibu's dazzling sunsets.

Niles House I, 1969–71 Edward R. Niles, Architect

Since 1968, the year he moved to Malibu, Ed Niles has advanced progressive architecture and engineering in his work, creating some of Malibu's most exciting but carefully hidden houses, including one for Johnny Carson. Niles is the recipient of numerous awards and citations for design excellence, including a Sunset Magazine Western Home "Special Award for Expanding the Definition of 'House.'" Today, many Malibu locals regard him as their most important practicing architect. ○ Early on in his development as an architect, Niles had jobs in the offices of Modernist icons A. Quincy Jones (1913–1979), Craig Ellwood (1922–1992), and Carl Maston (1921–1992). And so in his work (he began his own practice in 1966) he has always shown a penchant for steel and glass. However, unlike the residential work of his primary teachers and many of his peers, Niles's residential concepts are not easily classified under a stylistic label such as Modern. There is a shared allegiance to articulation in steel and glass, but Niles's work separates itself as a result of his frequent harnessing of advanced structural-engineering practices. Because of this, his houses, not unlike those of John Lautner or even Frank Gehry, usually appeal only to the most daring of clients. ○ In the case of the house that Niles designed for this one-acre hilltop site, the architect was working for himself. He had purchased the Ramirez Canyon property with the intention of building his first house for his family. There, he created an eighteen-hundred-square-foot two-story glass-and-steel cube that was divided into three bedrooms, two baths, a formal dining area, a small living room, and a large space containing the kitchen and family room. Its distinguishing feature, however, was an enormous trapezoid-shaped roof, framed in steel and sheathed on the sides in milled redwood planks. Both ends of the roof had unusually broad vented overhangs that reached twenty-four feet into the landscape, creating large shaded trellis spaces and providing the glass facade protection from the ever-present sun. In 1982, the house caught fire but was saved and eventually restored.

1970s

Gillberg House, ca. 1970 Carl Gillberg, Designer

Situated 1,800 feet above the fray of Malibu's shopping centers and gas stations, the Gillberg House stands as an important symbol of the Santa Monica Mountains' long tradition of eclectic wood houses. Designed and hand-built by their creative owners—musicians, writers, painters, sculptors, ceramists—these simple houses, at least early on, were frequently made of redwood with a liberal use of locally quarried stone along with whatever materials happened to be left over from their owners' other creative inventions. Siting would prove to be everything to these Malibuites, however, as such houses are highly susceptible to sparks. Today, the tradition is on the verge of extinction as even the most remote properties here are valued in a range that is financially feasible for corporate tycoons and similarly paid entertainers. ○ Like a painting that is never viewed by the artist as being quite finished, the design of the Gillberg House came about organically over three decades. The beauty of the house today is in its details, each meticulously applied whenever its owners felt inspired. The form that one sees upon arriving at the Gillberg's is quite modest—certainly in relation to its breathtaking site. Next to Carl Gillbergs' studio and manufacturing buildings is a simple brown wood-sheathed ranch-type structure with extended shade-giving eaves. A reflection of the Gillbergs' appreciation for nature, large panels of glass have been added to every exterior-facing wall that can structurally contain them. Perhaps the most striking feature of the exterior is the hexagon-shaped wing wrapped in picture windows. It reaches out into the rose bush-filled landscape, affording the living room spectacular mountain and ocean views. A fieldstone path weaves through another portion of Chantal Gillberg's magnificent gardens to connect with French doors that swing open to a small foyer and a large formal dining room. Here, above shimmering hand-burnished concrete floors, more than a dozen reclaimed California-virgin-redwood beams, each about 150 years old, provide structural support and lend a rustic feel to a room that is finished with a wide variety of artist Carl Gillberg's highly sought-after works in ceramics, metal, and wood. A fireplace warms the room, the handcarved mantel and framed mirror of which are also the work of Carl. Its opening is outlined in rare original Malibu Potteries decorative glazed tiles that were added to the house after being found derelict in the basement of an old house in Topanga. ○ Through the dining area the master bedroom and bath as well as an outdoor shower and vanity are accessed. Fenced in and surrounded by flowering potted plants, trees, and more of Carl's radiant giant hand-thrown pots, the flagstone of the shower bed extends to a small field of Mexican beach pebbles set in aggregate. Adjacent to this natural light-filled space is the handmade vanity, a feature that is distinguished by a sparkling hand-thrown sink and mirror frame, also done by Carl. Around the corner is one of the most tranquil places in the house, the outdoor room with hot tub. It was created after a typically monumental hand-thrown planter that Carl had made for a client was given back to him after it had been determined that a different size was needed. Carl was then inspired to use it here to make a hot tub. The hot tub is faced in locally quarried stone, uniting it beautifully with the landscape. ○ The living room is another warm and inviting exhibition space. Opposite a freestanding fireplace and surrounded by Carl's hand-carved wood sculptures and tables, hand-thrown pots, and hand-forged lamps, among other Gillberg creations, are furnishings and decorative objects that the Gillbergs have collected over the years during their many adventures through South America, the Caribbean (Haiti in particular), Europe, and beyond.

Rapf House, 1971 David J. Flood, Architect

Award-winning architect David Flood began his practice in the San Francisco Bay Area in 1967, around the time when progressive architects across the country were beginning to incorporate into their work various iconic rural forms borrowed from America's colonial past. A direct response to the rigidity of the Modern aesthetic, this movement, eventually termed *Post-Modern*, made it to Malibu early on in its evolution via the progressive hand of architect David Flood. An understanding of the design of Flood's Rapf House will best be reached through a look at the architecture that had the greatest influence on its design. ○ Six years before the completion of the Rapf House, the influential firm of Moore, Lyndon, Turnbull, and Whitaker (MLTW) had completed a condominium—its first contribution to a five-thousand-acre planned community called the Sea Ranch. In every aspect of its land use, architectural design, and general execution, the Sea Ranch, a self-contained community composed of houses, condos, stores, restaurants, a swim and tennis club, and other shared facilities all situated right on the coastline, was ahead of its time. The housing was characterized by steeply pitched shed roofs and dormers and exterior walls sheathed in milled redwood boards. There were no trees around the expansive plot, only windswept meadows, so the strong geometry of the barnlike forms stood out. Inside the house, the spaces were dramatized by the architects' emphasis on verticality and level changes from room to room.

Windows were smaller than had been the standard in the living spaces of the Modern period, and they were used more sporadically. ○ By 1970, these beach houses were being heralded across the design-media spectrum, in part for their inventive reappropriation of certain aspects of rural vernacular shapes. That year, while the Rapf House was in development for its beachfront site in Malibu, a strikingly similar design by prominent East Coast architect Norman Jaffe was underway for the Perlbinder family on a beachfront site in the Hamptons area, in Sagaponac, New York. (It, too, would be completed in 1971.) The respective designs of the Rapf and Perlbinder beach houses would have been different had it not been for MLTW's Sea Ranch housing. Interestingly, at the time of the Rapf House's construction, Flood's architectural practice was primarily concerned with planning and designing multi-unit winter-resort housing for mountainous areas of the United States such as Vail, Colorado, and Stowe, Vermont. While situated on the beach in a barren location, the Rapf House actually faces a mountain range to the north. These facts help explain the house's distinguished profile: two steeply pitched mountainlike forms that connect at a valley in the east-facing facade. ○ As the earliest example of a design trend that, by the late 1970s, would be evident not only elsewhere in Malibu, but also throughout much of the United States, the Rapf House holds an important place in Malibu's architectural storyline.

Moore House, "Windcliff," 1971 James Moore, Architect

One of the primary draws of Malibu living has been its highly varied topography. When architect Jim Moore (b. 1924) went looking for a site on which to build a house for himself in Malibu, he struck gold: the very top of Saddle Peak, elevation 2,800 feet. Moore was familiar with the area, having spent many years in and around Malibu while an architecture student at the University of Southern California and, later, while working as a designer for William Pereira and Associates Architects (Pereira's award-winning firm would later design much of Malibu's Pepperdine University). Moore worked for Pereira until the early 1960s, when he left to start his own firm, Medical Planning Associates, which specialized in designing hospitals. The house he called "Windcliff" is one of a small number of Moore-designed homes, each of which was done either for himself, his family, or close friends. ○ The architecture of Moore's 5,000-square-foot house was, like the Rapf House, inspired by the architecture of Sea Ranch—which Moore had visited shortly before the first drawings of Windcliff were made—and the vernacular saltbox houses of New England. He distinguished it, however, by surfacing the shed roofs in COR-TEN steel with standing seams. The exterior of the two-bedroom house was sheathed in western white cedar. In addition to ten garages, Moore added a round swimming pool, which he made out of an eighteen-foot-tall redwood wine vat. A guest house was added to the property in 1973. ○ As was common in this particular style of house, the interior spaces were characterized by the verticality of their shed roofs and irregularly placed windows. In the living room, which was given a massive fieldstone fireplace, Moore finished the walls painstakingly in plaster, and he did the floors in twelve-inch-square Mexican tiles. The same tiles were used throughout the house, including on the floors of each of the garages. Directly below the windows of the kitchen and dining area, spaces that were finished with the same white cedar planks used on the house's exterior, the landscape dropped by more than 600 feet, providing spectacular views of the Carbon Canyon area. Moore recalled that the house was so high that, "it would often cast a shadow on the clouds below, which is supposed to be very good luck. The site was almost always sunny, even when the beach was foggy." Moore relocated to Tahoe in 1976 but retained ownership of the house for several more years. It changed owners a few times before all but the guesthouse burned in the big fire of 1993.

Davis House, 1972 Frank Gehry, Architect

Frank O. Gehry has been the most celebrated architect in the world since 1997, the year that his titanium-clad Guggenheim Museum in Bilbao, Spain, was unveiled. After Bilbao, he would continue to dazzle critics and the general public with free-form expressions such as the Experience Music Project (2000) in Seattle, Washington, and the Walt Disney Concert Hall (2003) in Los Angeles. Each of these extremely sculptural forms was made using computer software that had originally been created for designing airplanes. ○ Though it's generally not regarded as his specialty, Gehry has designed several influential houses including his own home in Santa Monica (1978), the Norton House (1982–84) in Venice, and the Schnabel House (1986–89) in Brentwood. ○ The Malibu house and studio for artist Ron Davis, one of Gehry's early works, sits on a three-and-one-quarter-acre horse farm. With its corrugated-metal cladding and shed roof (the roof is also covered with corrugated metal), the 5,600-square-foot house has the appearance of a large barn—perfectly appropriate to its site. Ostensibly done to tie the house to the landscape, Gehry even pitched the roof in accordance with the descending line of the site. ○ At the time of the Davis House's construction, corrugated metal was not a commonly used material on the faces of homes. In fact, it had no documented history of domestic utilization at this sophisticated level. (Gehry's first documented public use of corrugated metal in his work came about in 1968 for an exhibition at the Los Angeles County Museum of Art.) ○ For the Davis's Malibu farm property, Gehry took the concept of the Post-Modern shed-roofed house, then in its infancy as a trendy design, and subjected it to the kind of top-to-bottom reinvention for which he would become known. First he ripped away the idea of its board sheathing, a material feature that had given the form a sense of warmth and a connection with its natural surroundings, replacing it with a thin layer of textured metal. Adding greater "complexity and contradiction" to the design, he transformed the basic sectional shape into a single trapezoid, effectively depleting the house of perspective at its corners. Irregularly patterned sections of the facade and roof were cut out to accommodate picture windows and skylights that bathed portions of the interior in natural light while casting abstract shadow lines across the living space. ○ Spatially, the interior was given a markedly open loftlike character. (In 2003, designer Michael Lee remodeled certain areas for new owners.) Beyond the massive centrally pivoted glazed front door and dispersed between two stories are a series of public and private spaces that are connected by walls that have been deconstructed into irregular shapes and heights. On the ground floor, the foyer leads to a hallway that reaches into the core of the house. Here, on one side Gehry placed the formal living room with its fireplace and soaring seventeen-foot-high ceilings. On the other side of the hallway is an elevated balconied container that holds the den and an office. It overlooks the kitchen and the open double-height dining area that lies just off the living room. Both of these spaces back-up to the rear of the house and can be opened to the yucca tree-bordered patio and swimming pool by a series of sliding glass doors that extend across the rear elevation. Above pine plank floors (the planks are recycled construction scaffolding) are enormous wood structural beams that emphasize the unusual and dramatic roofline.

La Vigile, 1973 Jana Meek, Designer

Around the same time that Frank Gehry was inspecting the finished construction of his Malibu house for the Davis family, in the nearby Point Dume area of Malibu, a designer named Jana Meek was transforming an old Spanish Colonial Revival-style house into what would become her singular vision of a dream home. She would do it in a style that she would call "Ecclesiastical/Cedar Gothic." ○ The house had a breathtaking site, positioned on one-and-one-third acres near the edge of an eighty-foot sandstone cliff with some of the finest views in Malibu. Meek wanted it to have a strong sense of entry, so she added a thirty-five-foot bell tower to the original one-story structure, creating a triple-height foyer. Staggered around the perimeter of the tower, she placed a series of six-foot-tall rectangular windows made of hand-blown amber cathedral glass. To give access to the views from the tower's peak, she designed a dramatic staircase, which was made of hand-forged iron by Malibu artist Carl Gillberg. For the interior walls of the tower, as in the rest of the rooms of the house, Meek chose milled cedar. In the living room, the posts and beams were left exposed to show off decorative hand-forged iron strap anchors, also designed by Meek and made by Gillberg. ○ The surface materials of the house's exterior were also changed. The original red tile roof, for example, was replaced with cedar shakes, while the white stucco wall finish was changed to boards of rough-sawn cedar. Eventually, the exterior woodwork was painted to match the color of the sandstone in the surrounding landscape. Every room had access to the carefully maintained garden areas or the site's spectacular views, as oversized sliding glass doors were placed all the way around the five-bedroom, five-bathroom house.

Nauert "Phoenix" House, 1975–80 Buff and Hensman, Architects

This late-Modern textured stucco-faced house (1978–80) by Buff and Hensman is actually a slightly altered reincarnation of an earlier redwood–sheathed Buff and Hensman design (1975–77) that tragically burned on this site in the fire of October 22, 1978. Built by Malibuite Randy Nauert, the present home was given its name by architect Donald Hensman because the new house had risen from the ashes of the fire. o Buff and Hensman's simple but very effective design consists of two wood-framed cubes that are united by a covered bridge. It is a small house but the plan makes very efficient use of the verticality of the space, giving it a much bigger feel. The larger cube, a 1,800-square-foot two-story space that is oriented to the south, contains at the first-floor level the foyer, double-height living room and dining room with fireplace, and separate kitchen. The second floor contains a balconied loft space, now used as a studio, which extends the full length of the building and overlooks the living room and dining room. At the sides of the house, recessed into the facade are large panels of fixed glass that are positioned atop glass-paneled doors, affording the living areas abundant sunlight and easy access to fresh air and the landscape. Connecting with the living room is the covered bridge, which is walled in glass and also has a skylight. The bridge leads dramatically to the 500-square-foot small cube. It contains the bedroom and bathroom with large soak tub.

Beyer–Zell House, 1975–83 John Lautner, Architect

John Lautner's fifth Malibu house (see pages 104–111 for his first) took eight years to complete. Under different circumstances, it could have been done in eight months. The delays were caused by what has frequently been a roadblock to homeowners and architects attempting to create coastal dwellings along the California shoreline since 1972—the newly created, voter initiated California Coastal Commission (CCC). The CCC was formed in response to the staggering amount of new land development along California's beaches in the 1950s and 1960s. It was set up to protect sensitive ocean habitats and monitor ocean water quality, each of which had become jeopardized in many areas of the state by the early 1970s. It also was charged with protecting coastal vistas and ensuring that beachgoers could access the ocean without having to cut through someone's living room. ○ The Beyers had hired Lautner to design a house that would sit on three lots at Luchuza Point, a gated community in one of the most desirable parts of Malibu. By 1975, when the process began, Lautner had developed a reputation as an architect of houses that routinely challenged convention. Lautner's homes were not easy to understand, especially on paper. Thus, the CCC members who received Lautner's initial design expected problems. ○ While widely regarded as one of the finest in Malibu, the three-lot site had its problems, particularly in light of the CCC's tough new land-use regulations. Directly behind its place at the point were other homes, some of which were at the same elevation. Lautner's initial design had a walled-in tennis court on the roof of the house. Had it been approved, the Beyers' immediate neighbors would have had their fantastic ocean views replaced by a wall. ○ The design that eventually won approval from the CCC does not appear to have suffered as a result of regulators' repeated extractions. To the street, the house presents itself inconspicuously; little more than a small portion of the roof, the relatively small garage and driveway, and an entry path can be seen. However, Lautner probably determined this very quiet part of the design, which is not indicative of the rest of the house. ○ The entry path eventually becomes walled as it leads to a series of steps that descend to a very private entry court and garden space situated below grade but still open to the sky. Once one passes through the glass front door and enters the foyer—this space has waist-high boulders built into its polished-stone flooring and concrete walls, and is elevated from the adjacent living room by a few steps in order to further enhance the entry experience—the procession dramatically concludes with a direct view of another grouping of boulders, placed right in the living room, with the Pacific in the background. ○ The home has four bedrooms, four baths (the master bath is larger than most one-bedroom apartments), a study, a music room, a maid's room, a gym, a lap pool and large patio, a hot tub, a greenhouse, a double-height living room with an enormous fireplace and panoramic views of the ocean, and broad ocean-facing terraces. (In 1985, architect Richard Turner altered certain sections of the house for new owners.) Describing the Beyer House's skylight-filled curvaceous roof in his book *John Lautner, Architect*, Lautner pointed out that, "The undulating, freely cut roof edge suits the dramatic setting of rocks and waves. This made a free and ungeometric flowing space for living intimately with the ocean and the site."

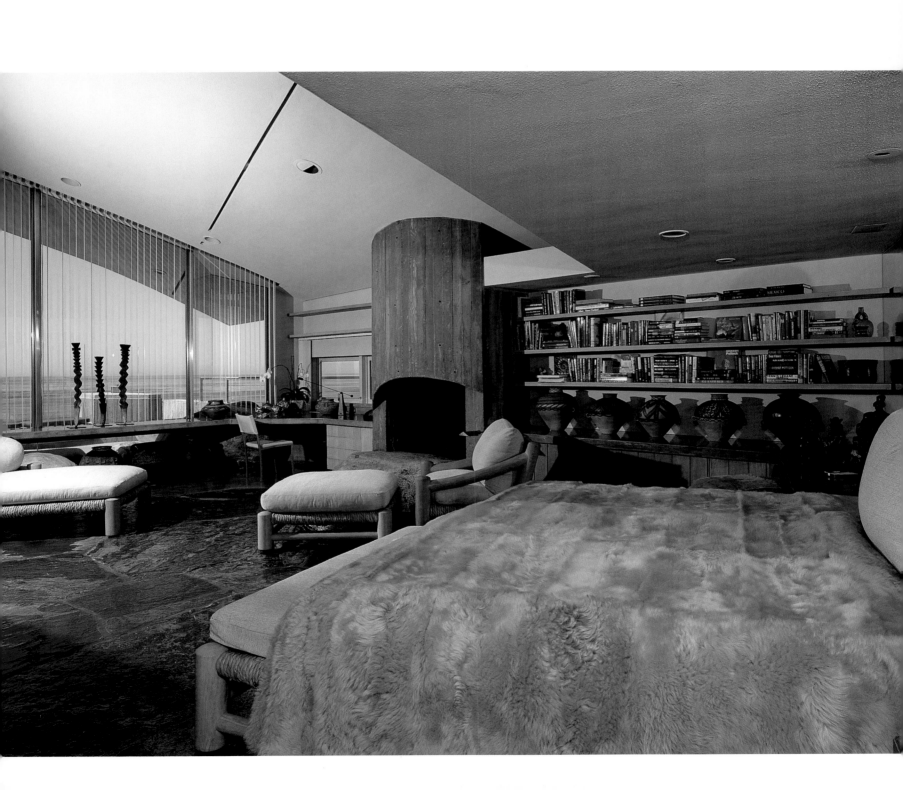

Hodges Castle – The Castle Kashan, 1977–79

The unbelievable 15,200-square-foot castle built by Dr. Thomas Hodges is Malibu's most notorious work of architecture. A drive through Malibu cannot be made without noticing the castle's crenellated skyline, astonishing mass, and perfect siting on the landscape— right at the promontory of a hill overlooking Malibu Lagoon State Park. Known today as The Castle Kashan, it is the private home of a real princess.

Segel House, 1979 John Lautner, Architect

Set right between the ocean and a noisy part of the Pacific Coast Highway, John Lautner's brilliantly singular work for the Segels would not have been a success without its large sound-insulating concrete wall that separates the home from the street. To further address the problem of noise, Lautner designed the walls of the house in board-formed concrete, finishing selected portions in warm cedar. The strategy has proven successful as the house has an air of quietude about it that one would expect to find only in a home set far from the activity of a main thoroughfare. ○ When they approached Lautner, Gilbert and Joanne Segel had certain requirements in terms of spatial accommodation, but they were willing to let the architect fully exercise his creativity in the process of shaping it. As Lautner later wrote about the house and its original owners, "The Segels had seen and liked a number of my completed projects before meeting with me. Open to new ideas and in possession of adventurous spirits, they clearly knew what they had in mind. What gave me the perfect initiating clue for my design was Joanne's poetically expressed feeling regarding my architecture: 'That I could stay on the ground and fly.'" Lautner's design for the eighty-foot-wide lot would accommodate a broad courtyard next to the garage, large living room with fireplace, dining area, open kitchen, guestroom with bath, studio, and master bedroom and bath. In the living room and in the master bedroom, Lautner brought nature into the house in the form of giant boulders, just as he had done at the Beyer House in Malibu (see page 156.) All of the interior wall surfaces are done in a combination of milled cedar and board-formed concrete. A swimming pool is situated just outside the living room. ○ In addition to its skylight-marked undulating roof form, a Lautner trademark, and huge frameless panels of glass in the facade (Lautner had them specially engineered to sustain winds of up to eighty miles per hour), the most striking exterior feature of the two-story house is its two giant arcing laminated-wood structural beams that shape the beachfront elevation and support the westernmost side of the house, where the chimney and swimming pool are situated. Lautner was at the house the day that Julius Shulman arrived to photograph it for him. In the picture that reveals the house's beachfront elevation, Lautner is seen standing just outside the curving wall of glass that separates the living room from the boulder-filled landscaping.

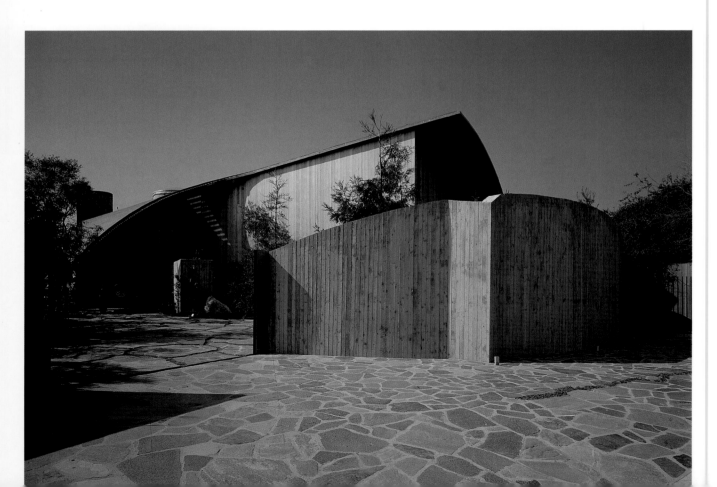

1980s

Streisand Deco House, ca. 1980

The world-renowned Barbra Streisand is said to be a great admirer and collector of art, various decorative arts, vintage clothing from a number of historical periods, and knowledgeable on matters of architecture. In the late 1970s, Streisand began what became a five-year process to bring to life an idea she had for a guesthouse that would be designed in true Art Deco style. It would be constructed on her compound in Malibu, a stunningly beautiful twenty-four-acre stretch of property hidden away in the Ramirez Canyon area, where she already had designed, built, and/or completely reinvented four other magnificent homes, one of which she often used as a recording studio. By the time she was done with the Deco House, it displayed a vast number of original Art Deco furnishings—some reclaimed from fallen Art Deco icons like the old Richfield Building in downtown Los Angeles, and others reproductions of classics. In 1993, Streisand donated the Deco House along with her entire Malibu compound to California's Santa Monica Mountains Conservancy. Today, the pristine parklike setting of Streisand's former retreat is open to the public by appointment.

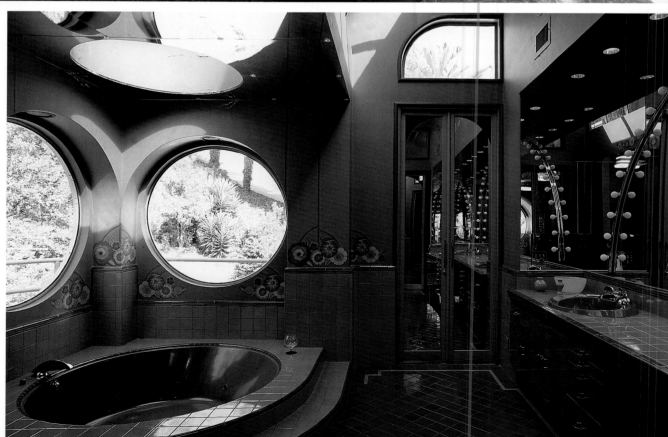

Roufe House, 1984 Marshall Lewis, Architect

Throughout the 1980s, Malibu architects, contractors, realtors, and bankers were catering as fast as they could to the spending frenzy and the "bigger is better" ideology that characterized Malibu's housing market throughout America's decade of excess. ○ In 1976, perhaps an indicator of what was to come in terms of the demand for architects in Malibu, a young designer named Marshall Lewis had just completed his first Malibu-based work—two houses, right on the beach—adjacent to Malibu Road. For any young architect, getting a design built in Malibu was a significant accomplishment. Lewis started off with two of them, and he had only been practicing alone for less than a year when the commissions came. Earlier, during the first phase of his career, he had worked in the Los Angeles office of Barry Berkus, now principal of the award-winning firm B3 Architects and Planners, and then on his way to becoming one of the most influential architects to builder-developers across the country. ○ On his own, Lewis has completed a total of twelve houses in Malibu, including the Roufe House in the early years of the booming 1980s. His work then was known for its sensuous, sculptural qualities, usually articulated in wood, brick, and stucco—basic materials that didn't dissuade conservative clients. For the Roufes, who were downsizing from their family home and would live in the Malibu house year-round, Lewis shaped a warm and sophisticated living space that continued the tradition begun in the 1970s of high ceilings, irregularly placed windows, and overall asymmetry

of design. This being the 1980s, this "downsized" home for two still had four bedrooms and four-and-a-half baths spread out over three levels, with each level having its own large sun deck. ○ The exterior was finished in stucco, redwood, and copper sheeting with standing seams. The house's many windows were done in tinted glass and set in aluminum frames. The Roufes wanted the home to be a reflection of one designer's creative vision, so they asked Lewis to handle the interiors as well. The front door opens to a small foyer and, beyond it to the left, the formal dining room. To the left and right of it are stairways that lead to bedrooms situated above and below the main level. A large cut-out in the wall between the dining room and living room permits clear views of the Pacific during

dinner. ○ In the living room, below walls clad in redwood, Lewis gave the double-height space a sunken conversation area with built-in sofa. Facing away from the ocean, the focus of this space is its fireplace, which he faced in a charcoal Italian ceramic tile. Throughout the house, the floors were done either in wall-to-wall carpeting, oak (only in the kitchen), or slate. Most of the lighting was recessed to reduce clutter. In the kitchen Lewis used a fiery ceramic tile on the countertops and gave the space its own breakfast nook with an oriel window and direct access to the second-level sun deck via sliding glass doors. The bright master bedroom has its own fireplace along with walls partially done in redwood and sliding glass doors that connect the room with its large sun deck.

Sidley House, 1984–90 Edward Niles, Architect

Ed Niles's house for the Sidley family is one of the boldest designs built in the 1980s in Malibu. Niles created a high-art spectacle that relies on steel, glass, and progressive engineering. The Sidleys and Niles determined that there would be a formal separation between the public and private spaces of the house. They also wanted to leave the landscape as untouched as possible. The living room would have a very high ceiling that would be conducive to music, and the house would have a swimming pool and an expansive yard. ○ As one enters the property, the driveway rises and then suddenly falls, setting up the elevated entrance to the thirty-six-foot-high hemisphere that contains the living room, dining area, and kitchen. Like the rest of the house, this unit, at seventy-two feet long, is made of prefabricated steel, reflective glass, and a special kind of translucent and insulated paneling called Kalwall, which has a moderate reflective quality and permits only soft, diffused light to enter the house. These materials change colors as the sun moves. ○ The formal entrance's oversized sliding glass doors open to an informal foyer, with the dining area and open kitchen to the left and the living room to the right, all of which is floored in a sandstone-colored tile. As on the exterior, the structural steel in the ceilings is exposed. Twenty feet across from the entrance, another set of sliding glass doors open onto the yard and swimming pool. At the far end of the living room, a suspended steel-and-glass tunnel ascends the other wing of the house—a gallery and a series of deconstructed spheres that house the guest bedrooms and bathrooms, library, and master bedroom and bathroom. The master bedroom has a small denlike space that overlooks the hemispherical wing of the house along with the yard and swimming pool. Each of these forms is raised six feet off the ground on enormous pilings. The house is heated and cooled by a system that relies on the swimming pool and a series of solar collectors that are positioned at the front of the house.

The Tree House, 1985–92 Randy Nauert, Designer

Surrounded by the dense foliage of its striking canyon site at the western end of Malibu, about 824 feet above sea level, the colorful Tree House seems to hover over the arroyo in which it is rooted. Set inconspicuously on salvaged telephone poles that have been cemented deep into the ground, the steady structure's defining feature is its original occupant—a large oak tree. Roughly two feet in diameter, its elbow-shaped trunk grows up through the floor and into a void in the roof that was specially designed to accommodate its growth and occasional swaying. The tree lives just off-center of the living room, and it is known to be a particularly noisy occupant when strong winds come rolling down into the canyon. ○ When musician Randy Nauert chose this site on his vast property for a guest cottage, his eco-friendly outlook led him to determine right away that the tree wasn't going anywhere; the house would go gently around it. Nauert, who also designed and built his own equally rustic home and office atop the adjacent hill along with a refined three-story hill-hugging Craftsman Style house at the other end of his property, designed the Tree House to be a real living space for visiting friends. Much like the working-ranch buildings of early Malibu, the simple single-gable structure is board-and-batten sheathed and strives to be unified with its site. Spatially the house consists of a living room, bedroom, kitchen, and bath, each of which open onto a broad covered deck that juts out over the ravine. ○ In the corner of the living room, next to the doorway at the patio-facing gable end, Nauert placed an old wood-burning stove. The antique can effectively heat most of the house during the chilly nights that are common at this elevation in Malibu. Picture windows were placed across the back and front, connecting the inside of the house with its surroundings and affording views of frequent visitors such as Heckel and Jeckel (Nauert's blind-and-deaf pigs) and wild coyotes. ○ Nauert gave the Tree House even greater design distinction by utilizing in its construction a wide array of materials from some of the architecturally pedigreed homes that he has owned. For example, the door in the Tree House's bathroom and all of its hardware were specified by the great period-styles architect Wallace Neff (1895–1982) for one of his early-1950s Malibu beach houses. While renovating the Neff house, which Nauert owned at the time, he replaced the materials but decided to save them for reuse.

Landon House, 1986 Tharp-Williams, Interior Designer

Michael Landon (1936–1991), one of America's most popular actors for his roles in television's *Bonanza*, *Little House on the Prairie*, and *Highway to Heaven*, purchased this triangular wind-cutting two-story on the beach in the early 1980s. About a year later, the Landons decided that the house needed a new look if it was to be an accurate reflection of their tastes and playful lifestyle in Malibu. Soon they connected with one of the area's most sought-after interior design firms, Tharp-Williams of Pacific Palisades. Joann Tharp and Mark Williams would spend the next two years thoroughly transforming the house's interior into a nautical-themed Disneylike stage set complete with furnishings made of seashells and driftwood. ○ The fantasy began the moment one entered the house. Protruding from a wall in the foyer was a large saltwater aquarium, which cast a brilliant glow on the walls and floor of the space. A few steps further in toward the unconfined space of the living room, right next to the spiral staircase with its ironwork done in a curling wave motif with iridescent glass infill, the designers created a rock wall that had water falling from its peak and an array of orchids growing out from it. In the kitchen, Tharp and Williams opened the wall that had always blocked the room from views of the ocean. The dining area, situated just off the living room, was given a low-slung oval dining table around which the designers positioned a circular sectional sofa for a more casual

and convivial dining experience. Due to the wall of glass set between the living and dining area and the outdoor patio, the house already had a strong indoor/outdoor feel. However, Tharp and Williams chose to further enhance the house's relationship with the pool, patio, and beachfront by applying the same textured concreted tile inside the house as outside around the swimming pool.

Rossi House, 1986 Ted Tokio Tanaka, Architect

Clinging to a precipice that overlooks Malibu's La Costa Beach, Ted Tanaka's beautifully angular Rossi House looks like a futuristic ocean liner that is awaiting the moment when the seas will rise up and free it from the land. The Venice-based Tanaka, who has been designing homes in and around Malibu since the mid-1970s and once worked for David J. Flood Architects (see pp. 129–133 for a house by Flood), is known for creating very modern geometrical forms. Influenced by the work of Modern pioneer Le Corbusier (1887–1965) whose designs often employed nautical themes, Tanaka is also known for handling not only design matters, but also the construction of his projects. ○ The Rossis wanted a modern house, and they were drawn to Tanaka's style after seeing a number of his works in Venice and Los Angeles. When they met with the architect, they put forth their requirements: three bedrooms and three baths, no hallways, and amazing vistas from every room. ○ Entry to the 2,500-square-foot home is made on the mountain-facing side of the breathtaking site. Upon entering the foyer—a space that receives natural light via a glass-block-filled section in the stucco-faced front facade—one is immediately confronted with the spectacular vistas beyond the glass-paneled walls of the living room below. To the right is a guest bedroom and bath. Directly ahead are a series of steps that descend a half level to the living room with its cozy bar area, dining room, and kitchen. Stretching the living room space out into the fresh air is a triangle-shaped outdoor patio, which is set into the prowlike corner of the house. Another stairway, situated off the living room, leads down to another guest bedroom and bathroom and the master bedroom and bathroom. The master bedroom has its own patio space. Granite was used in the bright triangular master bathroom, which has a stall shower and soak tub enclosed behind glass. Below the master bedroom level is another floor, which contains a large recreation room that connects through glass doors with the patio of the swimming pool area and the richly planted landscape.

Arnoldi House, 1987 Charles Arnoldi, Designer

The house designed by nationally renowned painter and sculptor Charles Arnoldi was built for him and his wife, Katie, and their children. It sits on Point Dume land that has been in Katie's family since the early 1940s, shortly after this part of Malibu was first made available for purchase from the Rindges. The Arnoldis come here to relax and commune with this beautiful place. With a site as visually arresting as this one, architecture can be disruptive to the experience. The challenge for the designer is to create a house that performs its functions while celebrating its natural surroundings. Arnoldi's simple light-gray concrete cube does this. ○ The house reads as a portal to the ocean. A single large opening in the front of the cube is repeated in the same position at the back, enabling ideally framed views of the horizon from the moment one enters the property from the driveway. The openings are set in the facade about five feet below the roof-edge to protect the artworks on the walls from receiving direct sunlight, and they have been finished with eighteen-foot-high sliding glass doors. In the front of the house, the doors slide open to give direct access to the primary entertaining space: the double-height living room with its polished and tinted concrete floors and massive fireplace. ○ The space to the left of the living room contains the children's bedrooms and bathroom along with a guest bedroom. To the right of the living room, on the ground floor, are the kitchen, placed at the front of the house, and the dining room. Directly above the kitchen, on the second floor, is a studio. It backs up to the master bedroom and bath. A large section of the master bedroom wall has been cut out to accommodate a six-foot-high piece of glass framed in wood that pivots open to allow the passage of ocean breezes into the room. The master bathroom is done in polished concrete throughout. A private sun porch extends off the master bedroom, just in case the direct views of the ocean from the bed aren't enough.

Martin House, 1988 Bruce Martin, Designer

Throughout the 1980s, the revival styles such as Monterey, Spanish Colonial, Santa Fe/Pueblo, and Mediterranean remained very popular in Malibu. Today, along the beaches and in the canyons one can find many fine examples of each. The Martin House, in particular, bears certain key characteristics of both Santa Fe and Spanish Colonial. Its designer, builder, and owner Bruce Martin, who moved to Malibu in 1981 and has designed and built a total of five houses here, attributes much of the house's design inspiration to the Spanish-style bungalow that he lived in as a child in Palm Springs, California. He calls his design "Southwest style." ○ Sited on a half-acre portion of a hill that overlooks the ocean, the 5,500-square-foot home is full of beautifully handcrafted features. On the exterior, the walls were done in stucco, all specially trowelled in order to give the surfaces a lumpy adobe look and feel.

Through the landscaped entry court with its koi-filled pond, a series of vigas—the exposed rough-hewn structural beams that are typical of the Santa Fe style—protrudes from the facade above the front door. Martin had them done in ponderosa pine logs, each knifed by hand in order to remove their bark. The vigas are also exposed in the living room ceiling, which features ponderosa pine latillas, the peeled wood poles that form the ceiling surface. An authentic latilla ceiling is composed of individual pieces of wood. However, Martin felt that the look was too rustic for the living room. He wanted the house to have a rustic appearance but in a sophisticated and clean way. Instead, he found a manufacturer in New Mexico that made thirty-inch-wide latilla panels. The panels have a tongue-and-groove edge that allows them to be joined neatly. From the foyer, the living room is sunken by a

few steps, and looks out through floor-to-ceiling glass at the backyard gardens and the ocean. ○ The dining room, which has the same gorgeous views as the living room, is floored in pink Arizona flagstone that Martin had cut into rectangles for a cleaner appearance. The same stone is used on the kitchen floor. The kitchen cabinets were done in quarter-sawn oak with solid brass handpulls, each of which was treated with acid to create an aged patina. ○ The second floor contains the master bedroom and bath, the latter of which was also done in specially cut pink Arizona flagstone. The master bedroom has its own small patio, but just a few steps away is an expansive trellis-covered deck. The trellis was built using Douglas fir for the trusses and more ponderosa pine latillas atop it that shade the space while allowing the passage of ocean breezes.

1990s

Rancho Cielo, 1993 Goldman Firth Associates, Architects

By the early 1990s, the intensive building activity that had characterized the 1980s in Malibu was finally slowing down. In homes such as Rancho Cielo, a house designed by the Malibu-based architecture practice of Ron Goldman and Robert Firth, there was evidence of a shift in ideology that placed quality over quantity. ○ Rancho Cielo, a two-bedroom, two-bath main house and separate small guest house situated on a two-and-a-half-acre plateau, was designed as a speculation property for a local developer. When Goldman first went out to see the site, he realized that seven very different ridge lines were visible. Also within view was an enormous rock formation on one of the nearby hills. In every direction, the vistas were striking. The architectural challenge, as Goldman recalled, was to design a house that would dissolve into nature. Like the influential Modernist architect

Luis Barragan (1902–1988), Goldman would articulate this idea by using layers of primary geometric forms done in stucco in colors taken from nature, all of which would be built around a water feature. ○ As Goldman intended, the 4,000-square-foot house reveals itself in stages. Five separate pavilionlike forms comprise the living spaces, four of which are connected via glass corridors (the fifth is a separate guest house that is situated at the front of the driveway to the main house). By dividing the living spaces in this manner, the architect was able to give each pavilion multiple varied exposures. The primary pavilion is situated to the right of a long fieldstone path that is lined with fragments of walls that border various plantings. It contains a foyer, dining room, living room, and the kitchen with its Douglas fir cabinets and Syndecrete countertops. Throughout

these spaces are walls made of large panels of glass and flooring finished with flagstone. In the dining room, the Douglas fir structural beams in the ceiling are left exposed. The master bedroom and bathroom are situated in the second pavilion. Both of these pavilions open directly to the infinity-edged pool and trellised patio. In the master bedroom, adjacent to the bed is a large panel of glass giving on to a grand view. To the right of this, Goldman placed a long rectangular window low on the wall in order to give the bed framed views of the rock formations. The third pavilion holds the family room and garage. The fourth contains a guest bedroom and bathroom. ○ From the moment one reaches the end of Rancho Cielo's 700-foot-long driveway, a feeling of serenity takes over. As Barragan once wrote, "Any work of architecture which does not express serenity is a mistake."

Cutler House, 1993–98 Quentin Dart Parker, Architect

The big fire of 1993 engulfed this Saddle Peak site nearly three thousand feet up, leaving only the concrete foundation of the Ted Tanaka-designed home that the Cutlers had bought a few years earlier. Tanaka had designed the modest one-bedroom, one-bathroom house as a live-in studio for a painter. This typically modern Tanaka design was still unfinished when the Cutlers bought it. So they decided to give the house a thorough remodeling and hired prominent local architect Quentin Dart Parker. About six months after the start of work, the fire struck. ○ After the fire, the Cutlers asked Parker to design and build a new house. In Malibu, especially for a complex cliffside site such as this, obtaining a building permit can often take four years or more. To avoid delay and structural-engineering expense, the rebuilding would have to be done on the original foundation. This was one of the challenges that Parker brought to his drafting board when he began to formulate his plan for the two-bedroom, two-and-a-half-bath house that the Cutlers had requested. ○ The glowing white contemporary form does indeed rest on the old foundation but cantilevered floors give it extra space. The living room, triangular dining room, dressing room off the master bedroom, guest bedroom, and each of the outdoor patio areas are raised over the sloping 1.6-acre site. Typical of Parker's designs, every room gives a unique framed perspective of the home's natural surroundings. The formal entry is past a large steel-reinforced concrete patio space, to the right of the sliding glass doors of the office/studio with its built-in shelving and loft. A glass door opens to a large bi-level space containing, at the entry level, a small foyer and, to the right of it, the kitchen with its stainless steel countertops and maple cabinetry. Four steps below this area, separated from the kitchen by a half wall, is the high-ceilinged living room with its maple flooring, special Syndecrete fireplace, and direct patio access. A natural light-filled dining area is situated off the living room. Also on this level are the master bedroom and bathroom, the latter of which is outfitted with a large steam bath finished in limestone. The bottom floor, which Parker had carved into the hillside beneath the existing footprint, holds an additional bathroom and a guest bedroom. For this room Parker designed a built-in captain's bunk and shelving. ○ Given the Cutler's experience at this site, Parker placed a sprinkler system on the roof of the house. It runs on an autonomous system that draws from a ten-thousand-gallon stainless-steel water tank placed on the property. Thus, in case of fire, even if the electricity in the house is cut off, the sprinkler system will continue to operate.

Kline House, 1994 Lorcan O'Herlihy, Architect

This is the first Malibu house by award-winning architect Lorcan O'Herlihy. Before starting his own practice in 1989, he worked as a designer for I. M. Pei and Steven Holl Architects, two of the most lauded architecture firms in the United States. Known for his inventive use of both off-the-shelf and experimental building materials, O'Herlihy was one of eight architects selected by the Architectural League of New York for its "Emerging Voices" program in 2004. O'Herlihy's Kline House sits on a hillside lot across the street from other multiple-story homes and Latigo Beach. In order to provide the primary living spaces with maximum views of the ocean, O'Herlihy walled them in glass and stacked the first and second floors atop a fifteen-foot-high concrete box that contains the garage, effectively placing the Klines' first floor at the same height as the second floors of the houses next to it. ○ The main house contains three bedrooms and three baths, a maid's quarters, kitchen, media room, and a single open space for the living room and dining area. The facade of the top floor, where the media room and master bedroom and bathroom are situated, is set back from the first floor to accommodate an open-air roof deck. Additional uncovered patio areas are off the living room and the foyer. Hidden from view is a circular towerlike guest house, now used as an office, that is accessed from the main house via a suspended steel-and-glass bridge. ○ The kitchen was given recessed lighting above birch cabinets and slate-tile floors. The master bathroom is also finished in slate tiles. In the living room, below an original 1935 handcarved mahogany surfboard by Tom Blake, are floors done in four-by-eight-foot sheets of birch-veneer plywood. The glass walls, sections of which have an opaque finish for privacy, are a special structural material called Profilite from Germany. This was its first residential application in the United States.

Cariker House, 1995 Edward D'Andrea, Architect

Ed D'Andrea designed his first house in Malibu in 1979, and has since added more than a dozen Malibu homes to his resume, including a 5,000-square-foot home on the beach for actor Robert Redford. D'Andrea is known for large-scale works—mostly estates—done primarily in a Modern-inspired idiom with flat roofs, lots of glass, and curving wall shapes borrowed from nature. The house he designed in collaboration with its owner, Jim Cariker, includes more than 12,000 square feet of living space and was originally planned for a 10,000-acre parcel (the land has since been subdivided, leaving the house with 3.5 acres) that sits in the foothills that overlook the eastern end of Trancas Beach. Cariker is a veteran builder and developer, and he wanted to build a monumentally scaled residence for himself. This house is his vision of the ultimate home. ○ The Cariker House, which includes a separate 1,500-square-foot office space above the six-car (with bathroom) garage, is a home for two people. In the main house, dispersed on three levels, there are three bedrooms and three-and-one-half bathrooms, in addition to a glass-walled round living room with fireplace, formal dining room, and expansive kitchen featuring red ash cabinetry, granite countertops (eleven slabs in all), and limestone flooring. Several thousand square feet of the home is devoted to entertaining, such as the pool table room that is situated just off the patio of the seventy-foot-long swimming pool.

Niles House II, 1995–97 Edward R. Niles, Architect

When Ed Niles designed a new house on property he had acquired at the western end of Malibu, wood was the first material he ruled out. Having seen the wood in his Ramirez Canyon home be consumed in the fire that claimed a portion of the house, he was not ready to use wood again. The living space—2,900 square feet filled with natural light—is composed entirely of steel framing (exposed inside and out) with infill of glass, including on the ceiling, and stainless steel paneling. Intended for him and his wife, the house exemplifies the architect's skill at integrating structure with nature in a fire-prone setting. ○ The fireproof single-story home is stretched east to west across the top of a ridge and is approached via a long uphill driveway that runs from the Pacific Coast Highway to a parking area and multi-car garage at the east end of the house. From here, a path leads through a grassy section of the front of the large property to an expansive entry court. The open-air court is framed by the house's structural steel. In the photographs, this portion of the house looks unfinished—as indeed it is. The structural frame was extended beyond the glass-paneled space that it contains (the living room, which is just off the outdoor court) in order to give the court a support system for the hanging of shade-giving screens, which have yet to be applied. ○ Glass doors are the final stage of the entry sequence. They open to reveal a sky-lit gallery that runs the length of the house, serving as a spine to the series of independent cubes that jut out and comprise the house's rooms. The centrally positioned cube holds the living room, kitchen, dining area, and service functions. The western end of the spine connects with the master bedroom and two bathrooms, the latter of which are walled in glass block for privacy. At the opposite end of the gallery, at either side of the spine, are additional cubes that accommodate a library, guest bedrooms, bathroom, office, and the garage. From every room in the home the ocean and the mountainous landscape are within view.

Ritenour House, 1998 Mark Mack, Architect

Lee and Carmen Ritenour took nearly two years to decide on an architect for the remodeling and expansion of their house near Point Dume. After a rigorous research process that involved a multitude of books, periodicals, and dozens of interviews, Carmen had become especially enchanted by the designs of Luis Barragan and his most successful follower, the world-renowned Ricardo Legoretta (b. 1931) whose houses are often characterized by pure geometry of form, exhilarating color (especially on the exterior), and special integration with landscaping. When a friend suggested they meet with Mark Mack of Mack Architects, the kindred spirit they had been seeking was found. ○ For the Ritenours' three-and-one-quarter-acre lot, Mack created an I-shape plan that seamlessly merges the original 3,000-square-foot house with an additional 3,000 square feet of new interior living space.

The exterior walls are faced in textured stucco and painted the kind of vibrant color—persimmon and mistletoe green—that had initially drawn Carmen to Barragan and Legoretta. Throughout the house, the walls have been partially deconstructed and the windows irregularly placed to allow light to penetrate the spaces from unusual angles. The site's landscaping, which includes plantings of penstemon, Bougainvillea, Queen palms, and bamboos, were done by award-winning landscape architect Mia Lehrer. ○ From the driveway, one can see the projecting section of the house containing a two-car garage and, above it, a space that will eventually hold Lee's recording studio. Also visible is the formal entrance to the home, set amidst a wall of large windows that can be pivoted open to bring in the cool ocean breezes. Beyond the entrance, a light-filled double-height foyer gives way to

an elevator to the dining room, a long hallway that leads to two bedrooms, a bathroom, and an additional studio, and a stairway that ascends to the second floor, where the architect has placed the house's primary public spaces. ○ Directly in front of the second-floor stair landing, beneath two skylights, is a half wall that spatially defines the maple-floored and marble-topped kitchen, which is openly joined with the dining room. Also on the second floor (to the right of the stair landing) is a long, double-height living room with fireplace with a wall of glass along its east-facing side that opens to an expansive deck. Behind the kitchen and opposite the living room is a family room, which connects the hall leading to the master bedroom with the nursery. The master bedroom has its own balcony overlooking the outdoor room at the back of the house and the wave-like steps that ascend to the swimming pool.

Benjamin House, 1998 Jerrold Lomax, Architect

Jerry Lomax has been an important contributor to California Modernism since 1954. That was the year he began working as a designer for Los Angeles architect Craig Ellwood (1922–1992), the celebrated Case Study House architect. Lomax had a dominant hand in designing Pierson House I (1955), Ellwood's second commission in Malibu, along with other Malibu houses by the Ellwood office such as the Steinman House (1956) and the Hunt House (1957). In 1962, Lomax started his own practice in Los Angeles, where he remained until 1981, the year he relocated his office to Venice, California. For the next twenty years, Lomax's Venice office (which later moved to Monterey, California) made many high-art contributions to the Malibu landscape, including this home for the Benjamin family. o The 4,500-square-foot house sits facing north on a manicured 4.7-acre lot in the mountains that overlook the Colony and its beaches. From the property's rose-filled front court, the design's three independent units are evident: two elongated smooth stucco-faced boxes, each twenty-two feet in height; and, between them, a steel-framed prism, the house's core, faced in Kalwall translucent panels (at the second-floor level) and the glazed doors of the formal entrance. As one enters the home, the central prism becomes a soaring double-height communal hall that reaches out into the landscape beyond the vertically interconnected volumes at its sides. Beyond the foyer are a series of steps that descend to the living room. Here, at the front of the living room, is a freestanding fireplace with stainless steel flue. Off to one side is a cantilevered stairway that rises to a bridge that crosses the hall to connect the second floors. At the back of the hall is the dining area, which has sliding glass doors that open to the south-facing outdoor patio, a space that is protected by a cantilevered sunscreen. Throughout, the floor is polished and sealed limestone. o The space to the right of the hall contains the kitchen with its padded rubber-tile floor, cherry cabinetry, black granite countertops, clerestory windows, and sliding glass doors that open it to the perfumed air of the front court. Behind the kitchen is an informal living room that is linked to the backyard and the ocean views in the distance by sliding glass doors. The second floor on this side holds a guest bedroom and bathroom, laundry room, and exercise room. Each of these spaces, like those on the other side of the house, has sections of its walls cut out to partially open it to the hall. o The easternmost side of the house contains, on the ground floor, the master bedroom with its fireplace and direct access to ocean views and the backyard through sliding glass doors. Adjacent are twin bathrooms, which share a sauna, shower, and soaking tub—all interconnected behind a massive glazed wall. An additional guest bedroom and an office are located on the second level.

2000s

Enkeboll House, "Dolphin Head Ranch," 2001 D. Wallace Benton, Architect; Pamela Rigney, Interior Designer

Architect Wally Benton of the prominent Los Angeles design firm of Benton, Park & Candreva was hired by his son-in-law to design this 3,700-square-foot home in the Encinal Canyon area. Enkeboll had just purchased an inclined five-acre mountain-top lot overlooking the ocean, and he wanted a house that would grace the landscape and appear to be a part of it. Benton, who has been designing homes for Southern California sites since the 1950s, accomplished just that. Frank Lloyd Wright's principles of organic architecture are evident such as the notion that a building should have as few rooms as possible, that its colors should be taken from nature, and that it "should appear to grow easily from its site and be shaped to harmonize with its surroundings." O Because the house would occupy a very visible site, the California Coastal Commission imposed restrictions on Benton's design, limiting the height of the house to eighteen feet and protecting the site's oak trees. However, the site was supplied with stone, which Benton could use. The large

stones became the dominant building material in the house, visible in sections of the walls inside and out. This construction used a method that had been created by Frank Lloyd Wright around 1936 for Tal-iesin West, his compound of buildings in Scottsdale, Arizona. The method involves creating wood forms at the desired thick-ness where the walls will go, placing the large stones into the forms, and then pouring concrete over the stones, allowing it to fill the remaining air pockets in the formwork. The wood forms are removed to reveal a smooth stone-and-concrete surface as seen here. O Benton set the house in an east-facing orientation into the side of the mountain, creating a multi-leveled living space in one story, which steps down with the slopes of the site. Past the boulder-strewn entry court and beneath a facade of stonework, stucco panels, and tinted ribbon windows, glazed doors open to a small foyer, which is adja-cent to an open space that contains the dining area and kitchen. Below cove ceil-ings, maple floors contrast with cherry

cabinets and large granite countertops. Behind the dining table, sliding glass doors open to a broad uncovered patio that offers expansive views. To the left, at the south-facing end of the house, steps descend into the living room with its stone walls, cherry cabinets, fireplace with heavily handcarved wood moldings, and floor-to-ceiling panels of glass that slide open to link with a large outdoor patio. Below the patio is a fieldstone path that winds down through the oak trees to a Jacuzzi, which sits at the edge of a cliff overlooking the mountains and the ocean. O To the right of the foyer, steps ascend to a guest bedroom (now an entertain-ment room), maid's quarters, and, at the very northern end of the house, the mas-ter bedroom and bath, which are wrapped in glass that unify the spaces with the site's foliage. Beneath this section of the home, carved into the mountain, is the garage and, further down, a wine cellar, the latter of which can be seen through a glazed section of the floor in the enter-tainment room.

House, 2001 Richard Meier, Architect

Since launching his firm in New York in 1963, Richard Meier has been designing public and private spaces to worldwide acclaim. Whether the Smith House in Darien, Connecticut (1967), the High Museum of Art in Atlanta, Georgia (1983), or the Getty Center in Los Angeles (1984–97), Meier's singular—predominantly white—forms always establish an inseparable relationship with natural light. This house (with separate guest house) on two beachfront lots in Malibu is another Meier triumph. ○ Both structures are built of steel framing filled in with enormous sheets of glass and white-painted aluminum panels. Like most Meier designs, the two buildings appear to change color throughout the day. ○ The two-story main house is entered through a grassy courtyard (it is part of a larger emerald green yard that faces the eastern elevation) that is situated between the guest house and the glass and painted-aluminum wall that divides the property from the Pacific Coast Highway. Entry through a double-height foyer reveals another Meier trademark: the vertical interconnection of all the rooms. Floating above this entrance point and lit naturally by skylights is a glass-floored steel bridge that links the second-floor bedrooms and bathrooms on the east side of the house with a private room for entertaining on the west side. In addition to ocean views from two directions (the room also has its own balconied outdoor patio), the entertainment room overlooks the yard at the western side of the property and the living room on the first floor. The kitchen is also on the ground floor, linked to the outdoors by floor-to-ceiling windows at its western end. Beyond the kitchen, below the curved wall of the second-floor entertainment room, is the dining area. At the very southern end of the house is the monumental space of the living room with its fireplace, glass walls, and sliding doors that merge seamlessly with the glass-shielded outdoor patio and the beachfront. Above each of the balconied patios are sunscreens and electronically adjustable louvers that shield the interiors from direct sunlight.

Lever/Morgenthaler House, 2005 Bart Prince, Architect

No matter what one's age, great house architecture can leave a lasting impression. Malibu's Mark Lever was only fifteen years old when it happened to him. The experience, a visit to the Bartlesville, Oklahoma, home of friend Joe Price, who in 1956 had built the first phase of a radically expressionistic design by the lauded American architect and educator Bruce Goff (1904–1982), shattered his notion of what a house could look like, and it never left him. Like most of Goff's houses, the Price House was aesthetically more akin to a fantastic work of Outsider Art than a house. Like a giant insect nestled into the landscape, it was enveloped in an eccentric mix of materials that included standing-seam copper sheeting and rubble blended with shards of glass. In some sections of the sharply angled structure any distinction between "roof" and "facade" was entirely blurred. Inside, the Wrightian (cavelike) space of the living room, for example, featured a sunken built-in sitting area, carpeting that was laid not only wall to wall, but also onto the walls (which were concave), abundant etched- and leaded-glass windows (each a geometric design by Goff) that were done in unusual shapes and sizes and unorthodoxly positioned, and a ceiling of varying heights, clad in wood in some areas and, elsewhere, in heavy rock-dash. Perhaps the most idiosyncratic house built in the 1950s in America, the Price House was not of the rigidly ordered, traditional ilk of the Paul R. Williams-designed Colonial Revival-style house that Lever had grown up in. This was organic architecture as com-

plex—beautiful yet imperfect—as life itself. ○ Nearly three decades later, Lever, who was now in his forties, found himself standing on the blank canvas that was the property he owns on Malibu's Point Dume and thinking again about his first encounter with Goff's Price House. He would build a house—his primary home—on this site, the kind of house he'd long dreamt of having. He needed an architect who could go there, however. "I wanted a house that, at the end of the twenty-first century, would still be an architecturally significant house," Lever recalled of his predicament. He eventually found his way to celebrated Albuquerque, New Mexico-based architect Bart Prince, whose award-winning designs (Prince has created his own design idiom that borrows from sources such as Antoni Gaudí, Frank Lloyd Wright, and Goff) he had followed—and greatly admired—since the mid-1970s, when Prince first gained national recognition, partly for his collaborations with his mentor Goff. ○ After Prince's visit to the site, Lever handed over to his architect thirty pages of program information—requirements of the California Coastal Commission, which his new wife, Alisa, an attorney, had studied, as well as personal needs such as a free-flowing floor plan that would be ideally suited to entertaining, numerous exterior decks and patios, natural light entering each room from at least three angles, and overall unification of indoor spaces with the outdoors. A call from Prince came some months afterward, inviting Lever and his wife to Albuquerque to see the model that Prince

had created of his design. The Levers were immediately sold. "It was as if he'd given me the ability to design like Bart Prince," Lever recalls. "Bart has the rare ability of taking the client and pulling him into the heart of the process." ○ Prince's still in-progress Lever/Morgenthaler House, the architect's only work in Malibu to date, is one of the most significant architectural works to be added to the Malibu landscape in recent years. The astonishingly inventive 7,127-square-foot living space rests on a roughly one-acre sloping lot just a short walk down a hill to a private beach. Prince's design comprises five bedrooms, six-and-one-half bathrooms, a separate wing containing four garages (three for cars, one for motorcycles), and a separate guest suite. Positioned next to the garage wing, a series of cubes finished in eucalyptus-colored smooth stucco, are six diagonal interconnected two-story squares, or modules, that reach into the back of the lot, each containing a different function and each stepping down the site at the same rate of descent as the existing hillside. ○ Upon entering the property from the street, the cubes of the garage wing and, to the right of them, the tallest of the modules containing the guest suite are immediately visible. As the photographs reveal, Prince left the structural steel framing for the modules entirely exposed and painted it a light gray, making it a visually prominent feature of the design. It shapes and emphasizes the windows and doorways and serves as trelliswork around the perimeter of each module's flat rooftop—areas that can also be used as sun decks.

Filling in the steel framework is, at the base of the structure, bare concrete block. Elsewhere are standing-seam sheets of copper, which will eventually acquire a beautiful patina from exposure to the moist and salty air and sun, and large geometrically shaped panels of glass. Each of the house's Fleetwood windows and glass doors slides open, enabling, particularly at the open corners of each module, a complete connection between the interiors and nature's elements. ○ The main house's glazed centrally pivoted front door, positioned at the lower grade of the third module, is just past the garage wing and the first two modules that, on the ground floor, are the guest suite with its private entrance. Marking the point of entry and emphasizing the house's special indoor–outdoor relationship is a glass-walled terrarium, half of which

sits inside the house, adjacent the stairway to the second floor. Next on the ground floor is the living room module (the only double-height module), which is open to the second floor, followed sequentially by the modules that contain the family room, study, and, at the very back of the house, guest bedroom and bathroom. Each of these spaces, whose radiant-heated floors will be polished concrete, is defined only by level changes and steel framework. Bordering the modules on one side is a gallery that, besides unifying the ground floor, leads to the butler's pantry, laundry room, kitchen, and, right between the modules of the family room and study, the dining room and the stairway down to the house's wine cellar. The kitchen, which is especially lavish, has a maple floor and includes a plethora of customized features: a built-

in steamer, rotisserie, granite countertops (including on the massive centrally positioned island that serves as a work station and bar area), and maple cabinetry. Just off the kitchen, past an eleven-foot glass door, is an intimate outdoor breakfast patio. Each of the modules will have concrete patios directly outside their doors. ○ The main house's second floor spans all six modules. Connected on one side by a spectacular inclined skylit bridge that extends the length of the house are, from front to back, guest bedroom one with bathroom, guest bedroom two with bathroom, the double-height living room, master bedroom, study, and his and hers closets and the master bathroom, the latter of which leads to a large balconied deck that overlooks the eucalyptus tree-lined back end of the property and the ocean.

**CONCEPT, PROJECT MANAGEMENT, AND
EDITING BY** Richard Olsen
COPY EDITING AND EDITORIAL ASSISTANCE BY Sigi Nacson
DESIGN BY Brankica Kovrlija
PRODUCTION MANAGEMENT BY Norman Watkins

Published in 2005 by Harry N. Abrams, Incorporated,
New York

Library of Congress Cataloging-in-Publication Data
Shulman, Julius.
  Malibu / by Julius Shulman and Jürgen Nogai ; intro-
duction by David
Wallace ; text by Richard Olsen.
    p. cm.
  Includes bibliographical references and index.
  ISBN 0-8109-5885-6 (hardcover : alk. paper)
1. Architecture, Domestic—California—Malibu. 2.
Architecture—California—Malibu—20th century. 3.
Malibu
(Calif.)—Buildings, structures, etc. I. Nogai, Jürgen. II.
Olsen, Richard
V. III. Title.

  NA7238.M26S48 2005
  728'.37'0979493—dc22

                        2004023526

Printed and bound in China
10 9 8 7 6 5 4 3 2 1

HARRY N. ABRAMS, INC.
100 Fifth Avenue
New York, N.Y. 10011
www.abramsbooks.com

Abrams is a subsidiary of
LA MARTINIÈRE

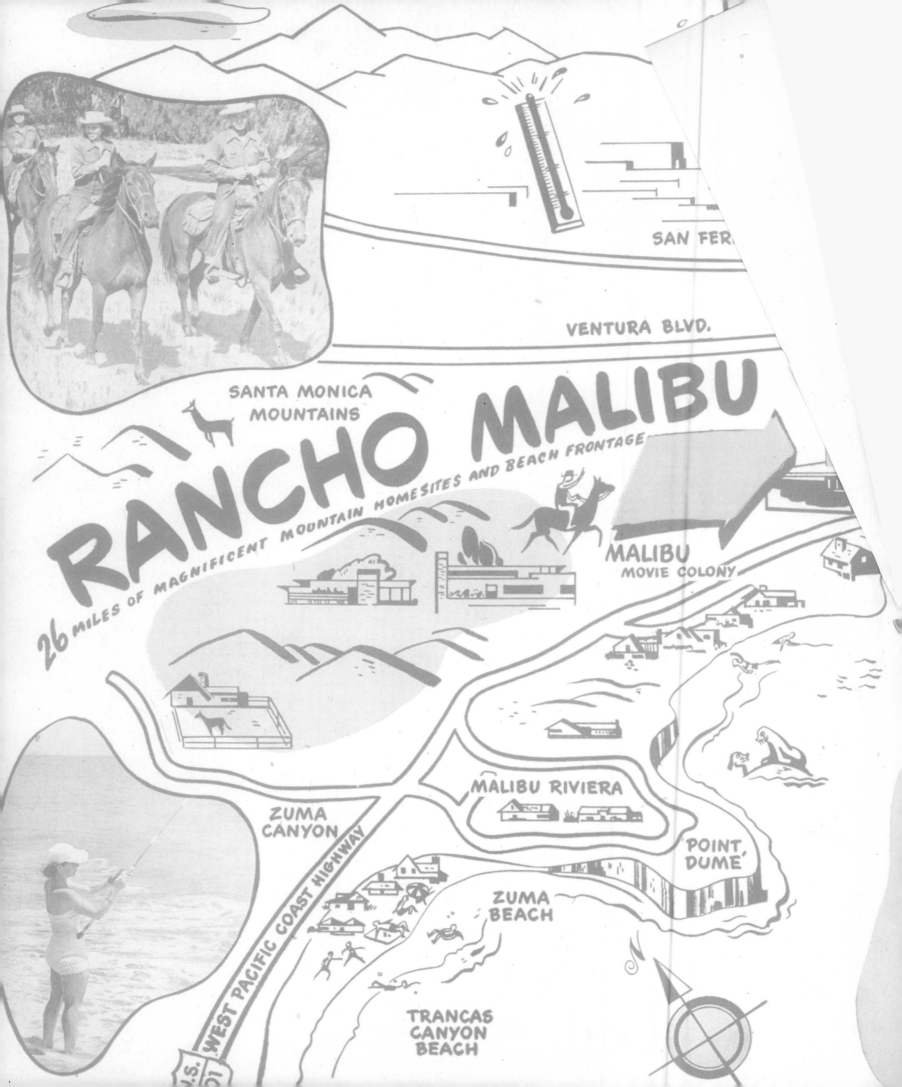

SAN FER[NANDO]

VENTURA BLVD.

RANCHO MALIBU

26 MILES OF MAGNIFICENT MOUNTAIN HOMESITES AND BEACH FRONTAGE

SANTA MONICA
MOUNTAINS

MALIBU
MOVIE COLONY

MALIBU RIVIERA

ZUMA
CANYON

POINT
DUME

ZUMA
BEACH

WEST PACIFIC COAST HIGHWAY

U.S. 101

TRANCAS
CANYON
BEACH